C. RUTH TAYLOR

FOREWORD BY
FAITH THOMAS

DESIGN TO WIN ROAD MAP

YOUR WINNING
LIFE AND CAREER COMPASS

Extra MILE Innovators

.   .   .

Published by
Extra MILE Innovators
21 Phoenix Avenue,
Kingston 10, Jamaica W.I.
www.extramileja.com
administrator@extramileja.com
Tele: (1876) 782-9893

.   .   .

Illustrations by
Norman F. Cooper

.   .   .

Cover, Layout & eBook by
N.D. Author Services [NDAS]
www.NDAuthorServices.com

Testimonials
from Design to Win
Participants

It gave me clarity on how I should go about my life goals and ways to get them.
—M. Hay

It boosted my confidence overall towards my social life, work and business life.
—J. Clarke

It expanded my mind and introduced me to a new perspective on successful persons.
—R. Kentish

Helped me develop the mental and social ability to go through life.
—N. Francis

It has encouraged me to be more vigilant and focussed in attaining goals by acting on them. The course is extremely useful for building proper goals and life-long positive habits.
—H. Spencer

It helped me to rate my progress whether I am improving or failing.
—N. Collins

It opened my knowledge on the importance of saving and to always make a budget so that you can spend for solid reasons and also to make long term plans.
—R. Robinson

My understanding of time-management and decision-making has greatly increased, along with gaining knowledge which will positively affect my experience in the working world.
   —K. Bennett

The topic, "Failing Forward," made me stronger, not to let failure bring me down but to learn from it.
   —K. Campbell

Before the course I was not able to deal with failure and rejection properly. However, when the topic was taught I was able to handle failure and rejection in a more successful way.
   —R. Burrell

It helped me to improve my lifestyle and character and to save and improve my income.
   —W. Dawes

I appreciate that it prepared us for the outer world which is the world of work.
   —H. Allen

To generations of Future Innovators
and True Life-Winners

NOTES

Scripture verses are quoted from The New Living Translation and The Voice Translation of the Bible.

For permission requests, write to the publisher at the address below.

Extra MILE Innovators
21 Phoenix Avenue
Kingston 10, Jamaica W.I.
Telephone: (1876) 782-9893
www.extramileja.com
extramileinnovators@gmail.com

FOREWORD

It is indeed an honour to be writing the Foreword for this excellent book, *Design to Win Road Map: Your Winning Life and Career Compass*. Ruth is the epitome of all that she has written in this book in which she engages her readers to develop a mind-set of "intentional planning" for their future, because she has tried and tested these principles, which have been honed through her many life lessons. She guides the readers in a step by step process to accomplish the goal of winning at life. This is not simply accomplished by purposeful planning, but also by having God at the centre of the plan: God as guide.

Ruth champions a wholistic and balanced approach as one engages life. She advocates balancing the physical, mental/emotional and the spiritual; as being lopsided in any area is detrimental to winning at life.

This book is an excellent book for those planning to start a career and for those who are retooling and redesigning their career path. In fact, it is a great book for anyone who wants to win at life. It provides very meaningful and practical tips and insight into the process that aims to help one win at career and at life. This is all done in a very open and frank discussion in which Ruth shares great insights from her own experiences, and also from the journey of her many and varied mentors. I have known Ruth for over fifteen years and have watched her grow on the path of self-discovery, and as a mentor to others. She is certainly a great inspiration to many, and is not afraid or ashamed of telling her story and sharing her insights. Her passion is to empower her fellow-travellers to grow from pain to purpose and to win at life.

I have taught career counselling for over twenty years, and this book is full of very practical insight and wisdom that I would recommend to anyone who wishes to win at career and win at life. It provides excellent life-management strategies in order to help one cope with the vicissitudes of life including failure and rejection. It promotes excellent time and money management skills. If your hope is to create a successful life and a winning career, this book is definitely for you!

Happy reading and happy implementing!

—Faith Thomas
   Director of Counselling
   Choose Life International

Table of Contents

INTRODUCTION

*"Life is a daring adventure or
nothing at all."*
—Helen Keller

"This is the final boarding call!" said the announcer over the intercom. "All passengers boarding South African Airways Flight 0204, from New York to Johannesburg, please make your way to Gate 3 for boarding. This is your last boarding call."

I made it through immigration just in the 'nick' of time. My breathing, now laboured, gradually returned to normal, and the once dry, white hand kerchief—now turned brown—was soaked with perspiration and make-up. Thank God, I made it! And now, with much trepidation and anxiety, I boarded the plane to join the scores of passengers who were departing from the familiar into the unknown...

Has this ever happened to you? Thankfully, this was just a bad dream. In reality, when I took my journey into the unknown in August 2013, I had more than enough time to board my flight. Due to careful advanced planning, there was no undue haste in departing from New York to Johannesburg. Nevertheless, that announcement is a familiar one made at airports all over the world.

Every so often, we find passengers hurriedly making their way through the boarding gate because for whatever reason, they were late. This can result in a great deal of anxiety and distress for the traveller. Sometimes it's even worse—the traveller is so late, that he misses his flight completely, which causes even greater distress! This is why airlines encourage travellers to be at the airport 2-3 hours before departure.

On the journey of life, we too can miss opportunities, and miss our desired destination due to lack of proper planning, and in many cases, we have to play catch up, because we did not get it right early. I believe we must practice the art of intentional planning for our future in order to maximize our chances of success in life. This process often requires that we think and act like a designer. It is the process of what I call "Designing to Win," and it often mirrors our travel plans to get from one country to another.

Now, let's be clear, designing does not prevent eventualities or delays in getting to one's destination, but it does relieve us of a certain level of anxiety. It enables us to make more effective decisions and take decisive actions in the present. When I travelled to the African continent in 2013 and in 2017, I experienced significant layovers and some flight delays. The trips however were quite rewarding. Life is very similar. Sometimes destinations are delayed, and we become frustrated when our goals are not met in the time we expected. We often encounter much turbulence and turmoil, disappointments, failures, setbacks and significant obstacles. In these times, it requires much faith, courage and persistence to continue the journey.

Nonetheless, I believe even with all these adversities that your life can still be a remarkable one. It can be remarkable because of the discoveries and the decisions you will make along the way. Adversity, says Ghandi, "is the mother of progress." Your life can be remarkable when you think long term and design a plan to get to that long-term destination. Your life can be remarkable when you not only design a plan but develop the habits and skills to actualize that plan. And finally, your life will only be remarkable when you do something to bring that design to life. These are the fundamentals of creating a winning life and career. These are the five steps in our *Design to Win Road Map*.

"Good planning and hard work lead to prosperity but hasty shortcuts lead to poverty" (Proverb 21:5). Although each of us is a unique individual with a very important purpose to fulfil, unless we become intentional about it and act and think like a designer, that purpose will not be fulfilled. Remember, life does not get better by chance, it gets better by design. Therefore, let's carefully **Design to Win** today!

PART I:
GET IT RIGHT EARLY

CHAPTER 1:
A VISION FOR YOUTH
EMPOWERMENT

The year was 2007, and I cannot remember much of what happened in that year, save for the fact of a compelling vision, which I received one Sunday morning in church. At that time, I never imagined this vision would blossom into what has become an all-consuming, heart-moving and enthusiastically exciting journey to start a movement to empower youths worldwide with the keys to win at life. I was 27 years old at the time and somewhat disturbed and distressed by the perpetual cycles of poverty, teenage pregnancy and spiritual under-development of the young people I had seen in my community and church.

It was all too common then, as it is now, that many of the young men and women in the inner city kept repeating the cycles of poverty, crime, teenage pregnancy and broken family lives, as had been the experience of their parents and grandparents. It was all too common then, as it is now, that young people would get baptised but never fully assimilate into the church and show forth the marks of true disciples of Christ. Within a few years, they would depart from the church. I believe it was these concerns that sparked the vision I received that Sunday morning in church.

While seated in my usual spot on the right hand side of the church pew, I saw an unforgettable scene in my mind's eyes. The worship scene in the church changed briefly for a few seconds, and I saw young people seated on the floor listening to me as I gave a motivational talk. I now realize in hindsight that this vision was the catalyst for the youth empowerment initiatives, which I would undertake over the next 11 years.

EARLY SIGNS OF FULFILLMENT

In 2012, five years after the initial vision, I started a personal development mentoring initiative for girls called *Daughters of Deborah*. Being an offspring of a teenage mother, I started this initiative to prevent them from becoming teenage mothers. I decided to use Deborah (Prophetess and Judge of Israel) and a cycle breaker as a fitting biblical role model to inspire them to become powerful and influential women who would bring change to their generation.

In that programme, I infused several personal development concepts which had changed my life. Originally, the mentoring programme was intended to run for one year, targeting teen girls (14-16 years). Nevertheless, despite my intent, the programme continued for two years, and the participants ranged from 13-18 years of age. Eight (8) girls and one young adult female (who was married) participated in the programme. At the end of it, they indicated that it was very useful and some of them wanted it to continue.

A year later, in August 2013, I offered a modified version of the programme to teens and young adults in Nambia, Africa, at the Samaritan outreach centre over a six-week period. At that time I called it "Designed to Win." Once again, these girls were of humble beginnings, and some were already teen moms. At the end of the period, some of the participants indicated that the programme was very useful to them.

Then in September 2015, I was asked to deliver a personal development programme for three (3) months to a group of eight (8) young men who were classified as "at risk" youths. This time it was a paid initiative and once again I modified the programme to fit the need. It was then that I made the final name change "Design to Win" to underscore a key notion that success is intentional, not accidental. Since then, the content of this personal development course has been offered to 370 persons at the time of writing.

Clearly, this is a growing movement. Thus, I thought it fitting to do an official evaluation of the course among the participants. This evaluation proved the usefulness and power of the programme. Their feedback has cemented the vision and the need to not only help youths on a small scale with this programme, but to deliver it on a national and international level and bring transformation to the lives of young people around the world.

GET IT RIGHT EARLY

It was in 2015, that I finally began to realize the significance of that scene in 2007. It was a picture of the mission to which God had called me. In that year, my speaking focus shifted through an initiative I spearheaded called "The Habits Matter School

Tour." On this tour, I was quizzically surprised to see primary school, high school and post secondary students listen to me attentively whenever I presented. In my experience, usually students will not stand and listen attentively without being distracted during presentations, but they did so while I shared. Two presentations in particular stood out to me: one at Pembroke Hall High School and the other at Campion College.

At Pembroke Hall High School, the students were rather unsettled and distracted as the devotional exercise took place. But after the teacher gave me the mike, it was as if a spell came over the students, and they all listened so attentively, that at points you could hear a pin drop. That experience left me quite intrigued and dazed but very thankful, because I was very nervous prior to speaking. At the end of the presentation, students expressed their appreciation to me without any prompting from anyone.

On the other occasion at Campion College, I was left in tears. The setting of these presentations was different. These were presentations to individual classes from Grade 9 to Grade 11. In one class, a student asked me why I was doing what I was doing. As I was about to answer, my eyes swelled with tears and I became emotional. The feeling of regret and failure had been weighing heavily on me for months, and now it all came back to me in a flood, making me very uncomfortable. I could feel the tears swelling in my eyes, and I felt vulnerable. After a few moments, I regained composure, and with deep conviction, I explained that my motive was to help them to GET IT RIGHT EARLY. On this tour, I was sharing lessons I learnt late in life. If I had learned these lessons earlier concerning purpose, self-worth and overcoming adversity, I would have been further ahead in life.

The statement "Get it Right Early" meant much more than I had explained to the students, because at the time, and the age of 35, even though I had a master's degree, had travelled around the world and had just published my first book, I was struggling to make ends meet. I could barely find the fare to attend the sessions daily, and all I had at the time was a dream and a broken heart. In that moment, I made a critical decision to purposefully empower youths to think and plan holistically for their lives and to teach them the keys to win at life. I wanted to prevent them from experiencing some of the unnecessary pains and regrets that I had been experiencing, despite my educational accomplishments.

As it is with most of our dreams, reality does not always mirror our dreams. My dreams and visions have always indicated matters that I should take seriously. With my training in career coaching along with the creation of the Design to Win Academy, and the Future Innovators mentoring, leadership and coaching programme, which currently serves a group of 30 young men (17-35 years of age), the vision now makes perfect sense. It is a call to Youth Empowerment which I can now chase more purposefully and effectively. This book will be a vital part of that process.

PURPOSE OF THIS BOOK

This book is a collection of the core strategies and principles which have changed my life as the founder of the Design to Win Academy. It serves as the main text for the Design to Win Academy and the courses and workshops which will be offered. *The Design to Win Road Map* is a practical tool to help young people between the ages of 16 and 34 years to set a better sail. This age group has most of our current Millennials (those who are between 18 and 34 in 2018) who are numbered at some 74.5 million according to the US Census Bureau (April 2016). Millennials according to the Manpower Group were born between 1982 and the year 2000. I believe it is best to start early in equipping young people with strategies to live an effective adult life. However, it is never too late to redesign your life to do your best work and to do what you love effectively regardless of age.

In my early years, between the ages of 17 and 30, I was on a quest for survival and meaning, but since that day at Campion College, I have been on a quest to live effectively. It is my aim to create both impact and income doing what I love, and to empower others to do the same while fulfilling their God-given mission and purpose in life. It is a quest to experience more fulfillment and joy in my life and work, and to help others— especially the youth—to do the same.

If your desire is to create a winning life and career, this book is for you. Whether you are a Career Starter (one who is about to leave high school/university or enter the workforce) or a Career Re-designer (one who has entered the workforce and sees the need to restructure your life because of levels of job dissatisfaction, personal pain or other life changes) this book is for you. *The Design to Win Road Map* will help you to walk in your mission and purpose, and give you the tools you need to restructure your life, so that you can progress with joy and fulfillment spiritually, professionally and personally.

HOW TO USE THIS BOOK

This book is a tool to be used to find and do your best work. If you feel stuck in life, this book is to be used to plan for your progress. It is to be used in the Design to Win Academy's coaching, courses and training workshops, and also by individuals or institutions for capacity building and personal and professional development.

It is a success toolkit which should be used in tandem with the book, *Keys to Win at Life*, which has 100 problem-solving and success strategies to handle everyday life challenges. The Academy is named after one of those 100 keys: "Design to Win." As long as you are considering your next steps in your life and career, this book will be very useful to you. If you are changing careers or redesigning your life, this book will be very useful to you. Furthermore, you can gift this book to others and recommend it for use by any of the following:

1. Family, friends, classmates and colleagues
2. Businesses and their affiliates
3. Educational institutions and non-profit organizations
4. Churches, community groups and clubs
5. Guidance counsellors, career development officers, coaches and mentors
6. In career development and personal development programmes
7. In student development and life skill training programmes

CHAPTER 2:
THE JAMAICAN YOUTH CRISIS

According to the Statistical Institute of Jamaica (STATIN) in its "Total End of Year Population by Age and Sex" report for 2016, Jamaica's population is 2,730,894. Of this figure 1,572,181 are 34 years and under. As you can see more than half (57.5%) of our population is below age 35. Any effort made to empower this 57.5% is critical –the majority of whom are youth and young adults.

Age	Structure
0–14 years:	598,413
15–24 years:	518, 453
25–34 years:	455,315
35–54 years:	675,417
55–64:	230,096
65 and over	253,200

According to the 2017 Statistical Report for the Parish Courts of Jamaica, the proportionately large incidence of male and youth involvement (18-29 age range) in nearly all types of criminal offences are quite telling from a demographic and social standpoint. These criminal activities include: murder, rape, robbery with aggravation, illegal possession of a firearm and shooting with a deadly weapon.

Moreover, there is also predominance of unemployment in this age group. According to the Statistical Institute of Jamaica (STATIN), Jamaica's youth unemployment rate was 38.3 % as of July 2014. This figure is close to three times the national average, which is 13.8%. The age ranges measured were 14-19 and 20-24 years. The high rate of youth unemployment is a major concern in addition to academic underachievement and lack of adequate training opportunities which tend to give rise to anti-social behaviour.

The National Youth Survey indicated that almost 60% of Jamaica's young people viewed migration as the answer to their desire to access opportunities for education and employment. It simply means that our education system needs strengthening, and there needs to be a move towards developing and improving our economy in order to provide better opportunities for employment and education at home. It also means that a sense of nationalism has diminished.

On a wider scale, according to a 2010 report from the CARICOM Commission on Youth Development, "homicide was the leading cause of death among males ages 15-24, at 19.8%. This was followed by HIV/AIDS, 13.6%, and motor vehicle accidents at 9.2%." The UNDP Caribbean Human

Development Report 2012 states that Jamaica has "the highest number of youth convicted of crime in the region." Internationally, another troubling statistic is that suicide is the second leading cause of death among youths 15-29 years of age worldwide. Homicide is the leading cause of death worldwide. These troubling statistics show that our youths are at high risk and are engaged in risky behaviours.

Is it possible to defeat these giant problems? I dare to believe that we can reduce the problem significantly, if we invest in our youths and challenge them to get it right early. Our youth clearly play a vital part in our nation, and what happens among our youth impacts the nation greatly. I firmly believe as UNICEF posits: "Education that helps young people develop (life skills) has transformative potential."

In this regard, there is space and need—despite existing programmes—for more efforts to empower our youth. The *Design to Win Road Map* with our career and life planning, coaching, mentoring and training initiatives will challenge youths to strive to contribute positively to national development, and this will open doors of opportunity for personal, spiritual and professional development. Although the task is daunting, I believe we can transform the nation one life at a time and one group at a time. If Jamaica's youths embrace and commit to the words of their National Pledge as a road map for their country, their lives will be better. The Jamaican National Pledge encourages us to work diligently and creatively, think generously and honestly, use the wisdom and courage of our minds, the strength and vigour of our bodies to serve our fellow citizens and to stand up for justice, brotherhood and peace.

THE MILLENNIAL CHALLENGE

Millennials, according to TIME magazine have been labelled as the "Me Me generation... lazy, entitled narcissists who still live with their parents." They are also said to be job-hoppers, unsatisfied with their work, industry killers, disloyal to their employers and have bad work ethics. However, this may be a misunderstanding of Millennials. The Manpower group did a global workforce analysis on Millennials in 25 countries including Japan, China, Canada, India, Spain and Mexico. In a document titled, "Millennial Careers: 2020 Vision, Facts, Figures and Practical Advice from Workforce Experts," they dispel some of these myths. According to the Manpower Group, by 2020 Millennials will make up over a third of the global workforce.

Contrary to these negative labels, the Manpower group found that Millennials are hardworking and over half expected to work past age 65, although a significant number are optimistic that they will retire before age 65. However, many of them foresee significant breaks along the way (84% of them or 4 in 10). They plan to take time out for caring for children, supporting partners in their jobs and in caring for themselves. Vacation and time off rank highly on their list of job priorities which also include: money, flexible working conditions, job security and working with great people.

Millennials everywhere say purpose is a priority. This was music to my ears as the *Design to Win Road Map* is all about discovering purpose and finding or creating a profitable job that aligns with your purpose. While job security is crucial for Millennials, they define it differently. Job security is more about having the skills to be employable. They are not job-hoppers. They want to advance with the same employer and are willing to work full-time to ensure and maintain their standard of living.

Millennials understand the need for skills development to remain employable. They value skill development and continued learning. 93% of them want lifelong learning and are willing to spend their own time and/or money on further training. This again is music to my ears, and step four of our *Design to Win Road Map* is about skill development. Learning a new skill is a top factor when considering a new job for Millennials. They want new opportunities with the same employer, not the next one.

Remarkably, three quarters of Millennials are working in full-time jobs. Though they favour full-time work, over half say they are open to non-traditional forms of employment in the future—freelance, gig work or portfolio careers with multiple jobs. Self-employment is also a tempting future option. They will stay if there is better work-life balance, a clear career path, and if they are recognized by superiors and colleagues. They will leave jobs when they feel unappreciated. Finally, Millennials possess the ability to quickly grow and adapt their skill set to remain employable throughout their working life.

In the view of these findings, if you are a Millennial, the *Design to Win Road Map* will be quite helpful. It will help you to carve out your career path and strengthen your desire for learning and development. It will teach you how to deal with the challenges that will come with work and life. It will enable you to do meaningful work aligned with your purpose, which is a core part of our winning road map.

CHAPTER 3:
INSPIRATION AND
CATALYSTS FOR CHANGE

THE GRADUATION EXPERIENCE

In July 2016, I attended my cousin's graduation from Kingston College (K.C.). He had just completed Fifth Form and was awaiting his Caribbean Examination Council (CXC) results to determine his next step in life. As I sat in the graduation ceremony at the Jamaica Conference Center, I was very impressed with the dignity, pride and confidence of the K.C. boys. They walked with their shoulders held back and head high, were disciplined in their demeanour and yet playful.

The speaker at the graduation was Delano Franklyn, a Jamaican attorney and old K.C. boy. He spoke in glowing terms of his desire to attend K.C. from an early age, and how pleased he was to have attended this noble institution founded by Bishop Percival Gibson. I was amazed and in awe of the Bishop's enduring legacy and vision, which was repeated and reinforced these many years long after his passing. All the K.C. boys seemed very familiar with the history of their school and the founder's vision.

The room that day was filled to capacity and, during the ceremony, it dawned on me that many of these boys were not clear about their next steps in life. Right there and then, a vision flashed across my eyes of a similar meeting at the Jamaica Conference Centre, but this time it would be a Conference with a thousand youths (Fifth and Sixth Formers), teaching them how to prepare for their next step and design a plan for the next 5 years of their life. I wanted them to **Get It Right Early**, so that what happened to me at age 35 would not happen to them. The vision seemed ambitious, and I wondered how I would ever pull it off. Now, I am beginning to see signs of how through the Design to Win Academy this vision will come to pass.

MEN OF FAITH, MEN OF THE WORLD

I believe that graduation was the seed bed for the idea behind the Design to Win Academy. I wanted to emulate the footsteps of Bishop Percival Gibson, who like me, was an educator and a minister, and one who contributed greatly to national development. He founded not only Kingston College but also the Bishop Gibson High School for Girls.

There is another notable Jamaican minister and educator who equally inspired me on this path to change—Father Hugh Sherlock (co-author of Jamaica's National Pledge and Anthem and founder of the YMCA and Boys Town Sports Club). Father Hugh Sherlock's penning of the National Pledge was a divine stroke of genius. This pledge not only serves as an incredible map for the nation but also a platform for change. The last lines of the pledge speak to Jamaica, under God, increasing in beauty, fellowship and prosperity and playing her part in advancing the welfare of the whole human race. Those lines represent my mission and synergizes beautifully with the Great Commission of Jesus to make disciples of all nations.

As a Jamaican Christian, I have a national and a global calling. Every Jamaican who repeats this pledge has a national and a global calling. No wonder Jamaicans are found in every nook and cranny of the world despite our small number! No wonder this little dot on the map has become a famous brand throughout the world!

What's more, in late 2017, I was introduced to a book, *What Colour is Your Parachute*, while I completed my Career Coaching certificate. The story of this book and its author further cemented the belief that as a Christian, I too, can contribute meaningfully to global development despite my religion. Its author Richard Bolles, who died in 2017, was a former Episcopalian minister. He was a graduate of Massachusetts Institute of Technology and Harvard University. His book and the strategies he created on job-hunting have impacted over 10 million people worldwide. His method of job-hunting and career counselling moved beyond the church into the market places and has transformed the lives of the religious and non-religious.

Similarly to these men, I desire to use my gifts through the Design to Win Academy to impact not only the church community but my nation and the nations of the world. These men were catalysts for change among the youth. Father Hugh Sherlock and Bishop Gibson invested in building the character of young people to facilitate national development and social change, and thus made an invaluable contribution to the development of Jamaica. I am impressed by the fact that these men of faith made a difference on a national and international scale. It is my desire to build on their legacies and do likewise.

CHAPTER 4:
LIFE-CHANGE BY DESIGN

Here is a good question to ask yourself: Ten years from now you will surely arrive. The question is, where?... In 10 years we'll arrive at an either well designed destination or an un-designed destination... We don't want to kid ourselves about where; we don't want to kid ourselves about the road we're walking... Now's the time to fix the next 10 years... Here's what we don't want to engage in: disillusion: hoping without acting; wishing without doing. The key is to take a look and say, Where am I? What could I do to make the changes to make sure that I can take more certain daily steps toward the treasure I want, the mental treasure, the personal treasure, the spiritual treasure, the financial treasure?
   —Jim Rohn,
   Author and Business Philosopher

I n 2010, the principles of Design changed my life completely, and things have not been the same since. In September of that year, I was at a crossroads. What should have been an exciting time turned out to be the exact opposite! I was planning to be married for the first time and transitioning to a new life and career as a full-time missionary. My fiancé at the time did not understand my missionary zeal, and at work, I was being pressured to stay in my job. Despite the pressure, I was very convinced about becoming a missionary and nothing could stop me.

However, I was not as certain about my relationship as I was about my career. I knew something was missing. For months I felt very frustrated and unhappy but feared the consequences of a breakup, and I did not have the courage to walk away. These concerns weighed heavily on my mind and emotions until I began to lose my smile and my zest for living. I could slowly feel myself returning to the dark state I was in at the age of 17. But one night everything changed.

I was browsing through various videos on YouTube when I stumbled upon a motivational speaker by the name of Les Brown. He was addressing a very large crowd at the Georgia dome, and I was completely captivated watching this man speak. He said words that deeply impacted me, "It's possible... It's not over until I win." I felt tremendous hope from those words and posted them on my living room wall. On that night my hope was renewed, and I knew then that it was possible to overcome my hurdles to achieve the God-given goals and dreams in my heart.

Through Les, I realized that I was in a toxic relationship which could ruin my life, and shortly after, I found the courage to end the relationship. Soon after meeting Les, I met another motivational speaker, Jim Rohn, and learnt about the power of goal setting and how to practically set a better sail in life. Jim taught me that, "IT'S NOT THE WIND THAT BLOWS, BUT IT'S THE SET OF THE SAILS."

This lesson of learning to set a new sail after the storm was key to redesigning my life in 2014, in the wake of another broken engagement. On this occasion, after my hopes of marriage were once again dashed to pieces, God gave me a new vision/design for my life which has since set me on a path that has transformed my life and work. This new design is enabling me to do my best work with greater effectiveness, fulfillment and joy.

In your life and career, you too, will face many challenges. Some of these will force you to redesign your life and head in a new direction. I believe once you have a design (a vision and a plan for your new journey) that you can win despite the odds. Don't be afraid to set a new sail after a "hit." I am convinced that no matter how bad it is or how bad it gets, *It's Still Possible to Win!* You can *Design to Win* and set a new sail to transform your life and work, and even feel happier and more fulfilled than before.

LESSONS LEARNT ALONG THE WAY

Since redesigning my life, I have learnt many life-changing lessons, in addition to the ones previously stated. Here are ten which I believe are vital to create an effective (winning) life and career.

1. *Holistic Thinking, Planning and Development:* I believe we are tripartite beings consisting of a body (physical and material), soul (mental and emotional) and spirit (the God-conscious part of you). Our thinking, planning and development should encompass all three areas. Between 17 and 35 years of age, I primarily focussed on the soul and the spirit. I had mainly educational and spiritual goals which I pursued vigorously. I paid

very little attention to the body or the material aspect of my being. I made little or no plans for my financial health, did not contemplate retirement and made no provision to own a home. This resulted many times in being unable to afford basic amenities such as food and transportation. Nevertheless, God has been faithful. I have never been homeless and never went more than a day without food.

I felt ashamed when I reflected on the fact that I was educated and skilled, yet struggled like those who had no education or skill. I found Solomon's reflection in Ecclesiates 9:11 very true,"... that those who are educated don't always lead successful lives... nor does food come to the wise or wealth to the brilliant or favour to the learned."

On the other hand, there are others who veer towards the other extreme. All their material needs are taken care of, but their soul is impoverished and they are relationally and spiritually bankrupt. Neither extreme is good. It is of utmost importance that we plan well for both this life and the next.

Prior proper planning prevents poor performance. Strategic thinking and planning occurs when we have a vision of what is to be accomplished, and work out the steps to get it done. It means we don't act for acting's sake; we act with a focus on results. Many people had a vision of where they wanted to go in life as a child. They dreamt of doing one thing or the other but never pursued it. I believe lack of strategic planning and thinking is one of the causes. From experience, I know that one of the saddest things in life is to end up at an unintended destination and then ask yourself in despair, "how did I get here?"

Regret is indeed a painful feeling.

I want to encourage you to not only think about getting a job/career but think about **all aspects of your life!** You don't want to reach retirement age and have to work by necessity rather than choice. You don't want to spend two-thirds of your life doing work you hate and merely working for survival instead of significance. Most importantly, you don't want to work for only earthly rewards but also for eternal rewards. It's time to holistically design to win!

2. *Think Long Term:* This is a habit of successful persons. While we live in the present we must think and plan for the future. This need played out for me especially in the areas of my finances and not making preparations for my material future. As mentioned before, rarely did I think about retirement and saving for a rainy day. When I saved, I would find a way to spend it or give it away. This failure to think long-term resulted in unwise credit debt for years.

3. *The Art of Life Hurdling:* I have been hit by many personal storms: two lung collapses, financial challenges, broken engagements and other relational losses which threatened my very existence. I had to learn strategies (keys) to deal with these challenges of life—hence the book, *Keys to Win at Life.* I realize that if we don't learn how to deal with disappointments, failures and setbacks, we will not progress in life. These challenges affect our emotional health, which is critical to live a fulfilling life. If we are emotionally unhealthy, our life will not be fulfilling, and it can lead to our demise.

4. *Ongoing Personal Growth and Learning:* It is the investment in my non-academic education from which I am currently earning a living. It is my self-education which has created opportunities for me to travel to places that I never imagined. For example, I taught myself how to publish a book and, before I completed my career coaching certificate, I taught myself career guidance. These are not things I studied in school.

   In order to increase our value in the market place, we have to learn more. If we want to earn more, we have to learn more. If we want to become more, we have to learn more and grow. We will reproduce who we are. Personal growth is an essential part of achieving success.

5. *Progress Planning:* To act without planning is fatal. Planning for your progress is essential. In order to do this, I recommend planning in 1-5 year blocks in the following areas: career and business, family and relationships, fitness and health, spiritual development, social and community contribution, education and learning, and financial and material. To this end, I created a progress planning guide which I use yearly to accelerate my progress. Visit www.extramileja.com to download.

6. *Faith and Action:* It is my faith in God that has sustained me in the rough times. My faith is the source of my self-esteem and self-worth. My faith is the source of the innovative initiatives, ideas and content for the inspiring messages which I deliver around the world. It is my faith that fuels my joy and provides my overarching "why" for living. It is the faith community that provides my

biggest network and support as well as personal and professional advancement. My faith has taught me the importance of community. Nevertheless, faith must be accompanied by consistent action to attain success. You can't have one without the other. Our *Design to Win Road Map* integrates both faith and practical action.

7. *Success Models and Habits:* It is the stories and examples of biblical and contemporary role models that keep me going in the rough times. It is the adoption of their habits which has fuelled my progress. On the biblical side besides Jesus-the Christ, other models include: Ruth, David, Paul, Boaz and Rahab. On the contemporary side: My mother, Les Brown, Brian Tracy, John Maxwell, Zig Ziglar, Joyce Meyer, Sarah Jakes Roberts and T.D. Jakes continually inspire me. When you don't know the way, examples are powerful templates to create a winning life and career.

8. *Live Purposefully and Effectively:* Our aim in life should not just be to fulfil our purpose but also to live effectively. We need to make our days count, however long or short they may be. We must remember the Purpose Giver/Missioner in all we do and seek his Kingdom first. I realized up until age 35, that I was very purpose driven, doing a lot of activities related to my purpose, but I was not living effectively. I was a broken person chasing purpose.

You know you are not living effectively when you are still struggling to put food on your table despite all the blessings you have received. You know you are not living effectively when you keep making poor choices in relationships. You know you are not living effectively when you are emotionally unhealthy. It is important to live effectively in this life while we prepare for the next.

9. *Association:* You become like the people with whom you most associate. In order to progress, you must find the right group and develop the right relationships to win. The bottom line is that you will never know or access certain opportunities if you are outside of particular environments. Your network is important. You have to leave your comfort zone and be willing to reach out to progress. You have to network and collaborate to win.

10. *Attitude:* It is important to develop a positive attitude to win in your life and career. As Zig Ziglar said, "it is your attitude not your aptitude which determines your altitude." A negative attitude will derail your progress.

CHAPTER 5:
THE DESIGN TO WIN ACADEMY

The Design to Win Academy is a **Career And Life Management (CALM)** institute built on the concept that life changes by design and not by chance. It is having a captivating vision of your future as well as planning to bring that future to life. The Design to Win Academy exists to empower Youths, Young Professionals and Go-Getters to win (be effective) in their lives and careers despite the odds. We will help you to discover your purpose and passion, and design your best life and work for greater effectiveness, fulfillment and joy. The academy also teaches fundamental life management strategies to help you to stay on the winning path. The academy is the primary arm of Extra MILE Innovators, a personal and professional development company founded by me, C. Ruth Taylor.

The Design to Win Academy is built on a theistic framework, because the Christian faith has played a foundational role in my transformation and progress. However, it is not restricted to persons of the Christian faith. All god-fearing persons, regardless of religious persuasion, can benefit from the strategies and principles that the Academy teaches.

The majority of persons who have taken the *Design to Win* course are not Christians.

We prefer integration like many of the early leaders in career counselling who evolved creative job-hunting ideas. According to Richard Bolles in *What Colour is Your Parachute?*, many of them were "from the beginning –people who believed in God, and said so: Sidney Fine, Bernard Haldane, and John Crystal... plus Authur and Marie Kirn, Arthur Miller, Tom and Ellie Jackson, Ralph Matson" (2018, 278) and of course himself.

The Academy teaches the **best practices of highly successful persons** and high achievers in various fields of endeavour, as well as simple proven strategies for personal and professional development, drawn from notable experts in the field like John Maxwell and Brian Tracy. The Academy embraces a **philosophy of hope and change** and a belief, that if we help people, especially young people to *"get it right early,"* that we can bring change to a nation. And with respect to my country, it will help us meet our Vision 2030 goal to make Jamaica the place of choice to live, work, do business and raise families.

I have found that Career Development is the perfect platform to blend my experiences as an educator, former missionary, speaker, career development officer and personal development coach. It facilitates integration because as Bolles notes in What Colour is Your Parachute? 2018 edition:

...the identification of Talents, gifts or skills is the province of career counselling. It's expertise, indeed its raison d'être, lies precisely in the identification, classification and (forgive me) 'prioritization' of Talents, skills and gifts... ca-

*reer counselling knows this better than any other discipline—**including** traditional religion... If career counselling needs religion as its helpmate in the first two stages of identifying our Mission in life, then religion repays the compliment by clearly needing career counselling as its helpmate in the third stage... And this place of job-hunting and all its anxiety—is the perfect time to seek the union within your own mind and heart of both career counselling...and your faith in God... (292-293).*

THE DESIGN TO WIN MANTRA

Our core message in the academy is that "You Can Still Win Despite 'IT.' This is our pledge to win, which participants repeat at the start of my live classes and in my presentations. This was inspired by Les Brown's presentation titled, "It's Not Over Until You Win," which changed my life in 2010.

There is greatness in me
It is possible to live my dreams
No matter how bad it is or how bad it gets
I'm going to make it
With Faith, courage and consistent action
I'm going to make it
It's not over until I win!

PART II:
HOW TO PLAN FOR YOUR PROGRESS

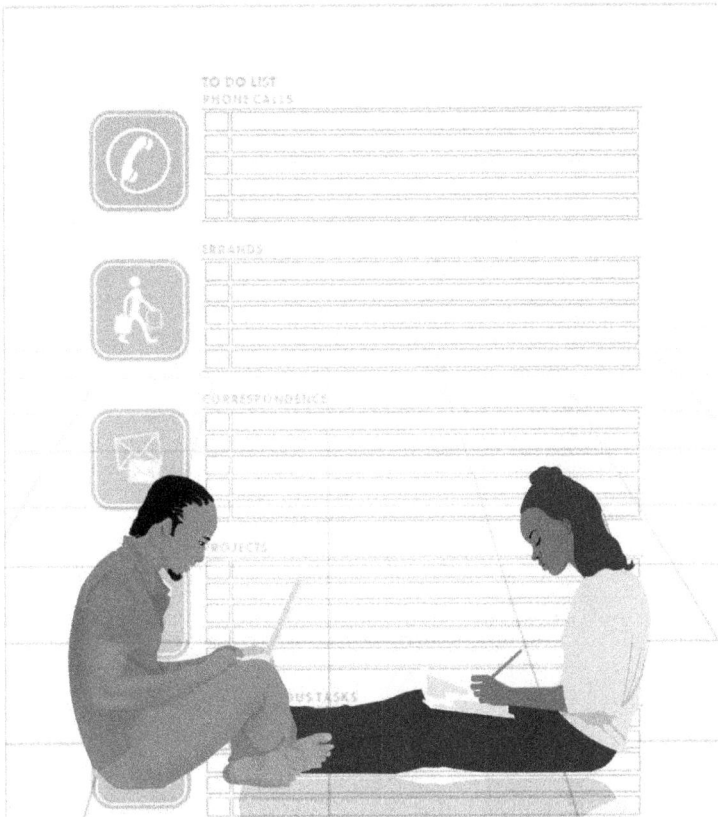

CHAPTER 6:
THE DESIGN TO WIN
PROCESS

*"The world is astonished when it meets
someone who knows where they are
going with their life; that is such a rare
kind of strength."*
—Dick Bolles

D o you want to progress in your life and career? Do you want to transform your life and
work despite the odds? Then, get intentional
about it! Many people spend very little time making
informed, conscious choices about their life and career, and end up with regrets. To avoid this, you
should Design to Win! It's time to design a career
and life worth living! If you intend to do your best
work and have your best career-life, I implore you
to follow the Design to Win Road Map.

WHAT IS THE DESIGN
TO WIN PROCESS?

This is a road map for change and progress in order
to win in your life and career. It has three phases,
and includes five steps to achieve the desired
changes in your life and career. These phases and

steps are built around three vital ingredients in our *Design to Win* recipe: *Holistic Strategic Thinking and Planning; Modelling Success and Life-Management Skills.* The metaphor of life as a journey is used throughout the *Design to Win* process. We use the acronym M.A.P to remember the three phases of the *Design to Win* process.

Mindset Shift: As author and motivational speaker Jim Rohn often says, "For things to change, you have to change." The first change that takes place is often in your mind, and when your mind changes everything changes. It was a shift in mindset that led me on a new career path after my second broken engagement. It was the thought I could turn my hardships into glory.

A shift in mindset is not only fundamental to initiate change, it is also vital to sustain change and continue to progress. Old belief patterns have to change and you have to continually monitor your thinking, and manage your mind to stay on the winning path. In this phase of the process, we identify the mental obstacles that threaten your progress and help you to develop new thought patterns for progress.

Actions: There can be no change or progress without action. In this phase, there are five steps (actions) that are required for change to keep you on the winning path. These steps shape the rest of the book.

Progress: Internationally renowned life coach Tony Robbins once said that, "progress equals happiness." We are often miserable when we are not progressing. To ensure progress, we usually provide a system of accountability to ensure that you take the required steps to progress.

This is a basic summary of our *Design to Win Road Map*. Let's look at the five action steps that are required to create a winning life and career despite the odds.

THE FIVE DESIGN TO WIN STEPS

1. *Discovery:* Conduct a self-study, life-analysis and self-inventory to discover your uniqueness (who you are), where you are now and where you would like to go.

2. *Decision-Making:* Determine your purpose. Make definitive decisions about where you want to go in life and establish what constitutes a winning life and career for you.

3. *Design:* Devise a strategic plan to get there (where you want to go). In our academy, we encourage you to create a 1-5 year plan since most people change careers on average 4.5 years.

4. *Development:* Take steps to learn more and grow. Learn the success habits and skills to get there. These skills include both technical and interpersonal career and life management skills. Our *Design to Win Road Map* gives greater attention to these five (5) Career and Life Management (CALM) skills:

   a. Art of Life Hurdling
   b. Productivity and Time Management
   c. Dealing with Failure and Rejection
   d. Being Money Smart
   e. Self-Management

5. *Do it:* Take consistent actions to implement your plan to get to your destination and bring your design to life.

Note Carefully: Although these are described as steps, they are cyclical and ongoing, because life is an ongoing journey of discovery and designing. As we journey through life, each day is a day of discovery and if we are cognizant of this, we will discover new things about ourselves and others. New decisions will be made based on the discovery of our uniqueness, and the direction our mission and purpose propel us.

Development will be ongoing. We will redesign during the different stages of our journey. And yes, as long as we desire to have a winning life and career, action (doing) will continually be required. Whatever is left unattended will deteriorate, and thus we must continually take action to progress and preserve that which has been gained.

Our *Design to Win Road Map* can also be summarized using the acronym DESIGN and WIN:

- **Discover** your purpose and uniqueness.
- **Decide and Design** your next steps in your life and career.
- **Equip** yourself with the right skills to progress in your life and career.
- **Study** yourself for greater self-awareness and clarity regarding your desired future.
- **Invest** in your personal growth to become more.
- **Increase your value** in the market place and **invest** in the lives of others.
- **Get** it right now to live without regrets.

- **Navigate** the course of your life better by using the Design to Win principles.
- **Weather** life's storms.
- **Intentionally** plan for your success and **implement** your plan
- **Never** give up hope in spite of life's challenges.

5 Proven Steps to Create a Winning Life and Career

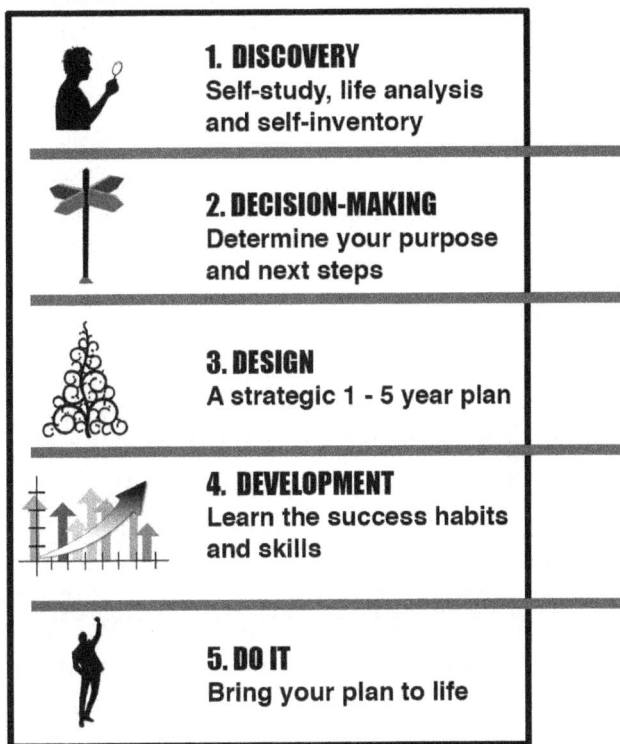

	1. DISCOVERY Self-study, life analysis and self-inventory
	2. DECISION-MAKING Determine your purpose and next steps
	3. DESIGN A strategic 1 - 5 year plan
	4. DEVELOPMENT Learn the success habits and skills
	5. DO IT Bring your plan to life

DESIGN TO WIN
FUNDAMENTALS COURSE

The Design to Win Steps are introduced in our course *Design to Win Fundamentals*, which is an online self-paced and self-directed 4-6 weeks course. *Design to Win Fundamentals* is based on Part II of this book. The course helps you to discover your purpose and passions and intentionally plan for your progress. The course comes with weekly email coaching over six weeks and one live 60 minute coaching session for greater clarity.

Although this is chiefly an online course, the course can be offered to small groups face to face. This course appeals to high school graduates, career starters and those who need to really redesign their lives and work for greater effectiveness, fulfillment and joy. Here is a testimonial from the first person to complete the *Design to Win Fundamentals* on-line course.

> *I was at a season in my life where I needed to put my purpose into perspective. I was asking a lot of questions about how to structure my life to accomplish all I know I am meant to be and do. That's when I stumbled upon Design to Win Fundamentals.*
>
> *This course has allowed me to think through some tough questions in order to answer the questions that I had. If you're in a situation where you need that structure at your fingertips, you can get the tools needed right here. If you are unclear on where to begin your life, DTW takes you on a journey from where you are, leading you with great clarity to where you need to be.*

My most impactful times were my coaching emails and session with my DTW coach, Cameka, where I was able to get a clearer picture of my own life from an objective perspective. Sometimes all we need is someone else looking through our window to show us how much is actually in our living room and how to organize it to its greatest potential.

DTW fundamentals will change the way you think about life and leave you with an insatiable thirst for growth and success.

—Jheanelle Foster
Online Course Participant

WHAT IS A WINNING LIFE AND CAREER?

While each person defines success (winning) in a different way, I believe author and motivational speaker Zig Ziglar's assessment, is a good tool to measure a winning life and career. He explains it as doing well in the following eight areas:

i. *Career:* doing well in a chosen field
ii. *Attitude:* freedom from fear and worry and having positive mental attitude
iii. *Spiritual:* peace with God, peace of mind
iv. *Finances:* Reasonably stable/prosperous and secure
v. *Relationships:* Happy and healthy relationships with friends and family
vi. *Personal:* Achieving set goals
vii. *Health:* Physical and emotional health
viii. *Hope* for the future

I recommend using a scale of 1-10 with 10 being the highest to rate yourself in each of these areas. Concerning the career criterion, if you are in school, being a student is your career. If you score 5 and over in most of these categories, I would say you are on the winning path.

Winning should be measured holistically. Winning is about fulfilling your purpose and using your best gifts and passion to achieve the life and career goals you have set for yourself. It is about standing in storms, bouncing back from adversity and maintaining your hope. It is turning tragedies into triumphs and birthing purpose out of pain. And of course there can be no eternal win if you neglect your spiritual life. According to Jesus of Nazareth, "It does not profit to gain the whole world and lose your soul" (Mark 8:36).

CAREER/WORK FULFILLMENT

The sad reality is more than 80% of people in the workforce dislike their jobs. This is sad because only when passion and purpose collide, can we achieve maximum productivity in our lives and careers. I believe where energy goes, results flow. It makes no sense spending two-thirds of your life doing something you hate. If you live a long life, you will be working two-thirds of the time. Why should you be miserable at work for two-thirds of your life? The *Design to Win Road Map* is geared towards helping you discover what would constitute a fulfilling life and career for you. It will help you to take the steps necessary to pursue your ideal life and career.

What are your criteria for career fulfillment? It is important that you pause to think about this carefully. Whatever your criteria, it should include doing work that is meaningful and profitable. It should be a mix of income and impact; passion, purpose and profit and enable you to have your desired lifestyle. It is work that makes life a joy and not a burden. It is work that makes you look forward to Mondays and getting out of bed each day. It's utilizing your gifts for the glory of God, and the greatest good, in a manner that makes you feel proud of your work.

In my case, career fulfillment is not only knowing that my work is making an impact but looking forward to my work at least 90% of the time. Ultimately, it is seeing lives transformed and working in a manner that provides the greatest level of freedom and flexibility, to enable me to travel and empower people around the world. This means that ultimately I cannot be tied down to a 9-5 job or the traditional working environment. It also means that I am simply not content to just work for money. My purpose must collide with my work and my work should be profitable so that I am not struggling to survive financially.

Career fulfillment is really life fulfillment. It's doing work that fits well with your core values, purpose, gifts, and passions. It is having proper work-life balance—affords time for friends, family, leisure and other causes. It's doing work you love and doing it effectively. A fulfilling life and career is a winning life and career. Our *Design to Win Road Map* is your ideal compass to achieve a winning life and career.

CHAPTER 7:
DISCOVERING ANSWERS

You are a unique person with creative ability who has been wired to accomplish a unique purpose and a shared purpose with the rest of humankind.
—C. Ruth Taylor

The purpose of this first step is to help you to:

- discover your uniqueness (who you are)
- identify where you are now, that is, your current reality, the dominant issues you are facing right now, what matters most to you and your pressing concerns right now
- identify your unique gifts and talents and to some extent where you would like to go in the future.

The chapters of Discovery will be a mix of a life-analysis and a self-study or self-inventory which lay the foundation for the other stages of the *Design to Win* process. You will also do a *Design to Win* survey based on your stage of development—Career Starter or Career Redesigner, as well as a strength finder assessment and the Kiersey Temperament Sorter personality profile.

THE BIG 5 EXISTENTIAL QUESTIONS

According to Dr. Eric Erickson's psychosocial stages of development, during our teenage years we struggle with the issue of identity versus role confusion, and we work on developing a sense of self. In young adulthood—ages 20-40—we struggle with intimacy versus isolation, as we struggle to form close relationships to gain the capacity to love. While I find his analysis to be true, these issues are not confined to this period. I know of individuals beyond this age range who continue to wrestle with these issues and their very self-existence. The struggle can be captured by five questions, which become the subject of each phase of the Design to Win process. Each of us throughout our life's journey, will ask ourselves one or all of these existential questions:

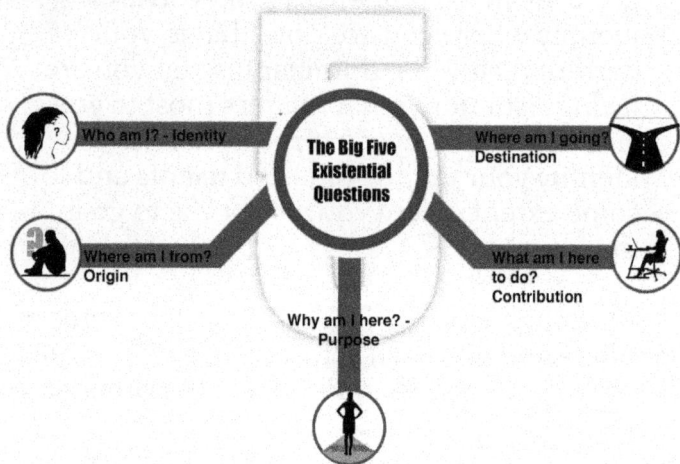

I began asking myself these questions at the age of 17 when I was in a state of complete disillusionment with life. I remember praying nightly that I would die in my sleep, and when I woke up, I angrily shouted at God, "Weh yuh wake me up fa? (Why did you allow me to be awakened?)" This struggle essentially dealt with: "why am I here?" and "what am I here to do?" It is in this state that two significant things happened. The first was an intervention in my life through which I received a vision for my life, which in turn led me on a quest to find out the meaning of life.

In my struggle with suicidal ideation, I felt unloved and insignificant and saw no reason to continue living. I even remember asking why long life was a gift and why do people want to live forever. It was at this time the first intervention took place. I was invited to a special church service, where three ministers, including a very wise woman, revealed to me God's plan for my life, which interrupted the story I was telling myself. Part of what they told me was that God was about to remove my timidity, launch me into a special ministry, and eventually I would travel all over the world impacting lives like some of the already famous ministers I knew.

Immediately, my life began to change when I discovered God's unique plan for me. Moreover, that wise woman gave me an important instruction from God that continues to transform my life. She told me: "God says to get more of my Word." This led me to an intense study of what I now know as the world's bestselling book: The Bible. I obeyed her instruction and in my study, I found answers that caused me to stop existing and start living. Through my study of the Bible I discovered my uniqueness. I believe you, too, can discover your uniqueness as I did—from the Bible.

Your Unique Identity

Earlier, I said two significant things happened to me at age 17, one of which was discovering that God had a plan for my life. The second significant thing was the discovery of my identity. This discovery led to my liberation from suicidal ideation and re-initiated my progress in life. I have always been an avid reader, and in that season, not only did I read my Bible, but I read other books, one of which was a book by Christian psychologist, Dr. Neil T. Anderson, entitled *Victory over the Darkness*. This book addressed the question of: who am I? Somehow as I read the pages of this book, all thoughts of suicide left me, and I have never returned to that point since (where there was an ongoing compelling desire to die).

The understanding of our identity, self-worth and purpose is the path to liberation and progress. I discovered then that my identity is very much about the person *I Believe Myself to Be*, regardless of my geography, family, cultural heritage and unique gifts and talents. It's what I am willing to accept as true for me. In my case, it became essentially about believing in who God and His word say I am: chosen, loved, prized and valued. Each of us is a unique person who has significant value and worth; born on purpose with a special purpose to fulfil. We are also different from all the other creatures in creation.

This of course leads us back to my first intervention when that wise woman told me to get more of God's Word. I discovered my uniqueness as a human being in the story of creation in Genesis 1-3 of the Bible. Not only that, but I also discovered principles of design in these same chapters, and I have taken the liberty to summarize the story in this chapter.

Now, I know that many persons in today's Western World no longer subscribe to the Bible or to the concept of creation. However, this is an essential part of the worldview that has transformed my life and gives meaning to my life. You, however, are free to choose another template to discover your uniqueness.

Having a concept of an original blueprint for life and success will help us in structuring our lives, inform us regarding the things we should strive for, and establish the legitimacy of that for which we are striving. It is the Genesis blueprint that has helped me in my personal growth and development. It is this blueprint that continues to give me confidence regarding my life goals. The Genesis blueprint has helped me to develop high self-esteem and a greater sense of worth. Finally, it has helped me to understand the ingredients for a winning life and why we struggle for success. I believe this template will guide you similarly and transform your life.

THE GENESIS BLUEPRINT

The story presented in Genesis, chapters 1-3, is the climax of the Great Designer's (God's) creative work. Essentially, it is the riveting story of how the first human couple's good life and relationship became altered forever. The picture of their good life is our example of the winning design for life. Their failure and the consequences of it are instructive in understanding our own struggles. Their hope for change and the promise of a better future inspire us to *Design to Win* at life.

WHEN LIFE WAS GOOD

The Great Designer, after creating the earth and populating it with a variety of living creatures—domesticated and wild animals, small creeping creatures, swarms of life in the sea, species of birds and lush green vegetation—made an all important decision. He said:

> Now let Us conceive a new creation—humanity —made in Our image, fashioned according to Our likeness. And let Us grant them authority over all the earth—the fish in the sea and the birds in the sky, the domesticated animals and the small creeping creatures on the earth. So God did just that. He created humanity in His image, created them male and female. Then God blessed them and gave them this directive: "Be fruitful and multiply. Populate the earth. I make you trustees of My estate, so care for My creation and rule over the fish of the sea, the birds of the sky, and every creature that roams across the earth. Look! I have given you every seed-bearing plant that grows on the earth and every fruit-bearing tree. They will be your food and nourishment. As for all the wild animals, the birds in the sky, and every small creeping creature—everything that breathes the breath of life—I have given them every green plant for food. And it happened just as God said. Then God surveyed everything He had made, savoring its beauty and appreciating its goodness (Genesis 1: 26-30).

As the plot thickens, we learn more details about the Designer's decision and how it was realized. We are told that the Great Designer made a man and placed him in a beautiful garden of utter delight and luxuriant beauty, called "Eden," and charged him to work the ground and care for it. He also made certain demands of the man *regarding life in the garden*. He could eat freely from any *and all* trees in the garden save one—the tree of the knowledge of good and evil. He was warned that if he ate of it that he would certainly die.

After creating the man, the Great Designer knew his work was not finished. He saw that the man was lonely and then set about creating a perfectly suited or fitting companion for him, who would be similar to him, made from bone of his bones and flesh of his flesh. He then brought this companion to the man, and the man called her **woman**, and she became his wife. His heart was glad, and they were naked and not ashamed. The Great Designer was so well pleased with his work that he ceased from his work of creating, pausing for a day to rest and enjoy his work. He would also meet regularly in the cool of the day with the man.

WHEN THINGS FALL APART

As with any good story, there is always a conflict, an enemy, a villain who tries to sour things, and so it is with this story. In this story, he is typified as a serpent. The serpent approached the man's wife and challenged her about the rule the Great Designer had given to her husband, which he had passed on to her. The serpent told her the Great Designer had lied to them about dying upon eating the forbidden fruit. With sweet words and promises of her becoming wise and becoming like the Great Designer, the serpent caused her mind to change. She subsequently acted in a manner that altered their lives forever.

The woman approached the tree, eyed its fruit, and coveted its mouth-watering, wisdom-granting beauty. She plucked a fruit from the tree and ate. She then offered the fruit to her husband who was close by, and he ate as well. Suddenly their eyes were opened to a reality previously unknown. For the first time, they sensed their vulnerability and rushed to hide their naked bodies, stitching fig leaves into crude loincloths. Then they heard the sound of the Eternal God walking in the cool misting shadows of the garden. The man and his wife took cover among the trees and hid from the Eternal God (Genesis 3:6-8).

The Great Designer confronted them about what they had done and then the blame game started. The husband blamed his wife, and the wife blamed the serpent. The consequence for their wrongdoing was grave: the woman's suffering would be increased. Childbearing would become painful, and her husband would become the dominant partner. For the man, he would from then on fight for every crumb of food, and his ground labour would not be as fruitful as before. From then on, he would eat by the sweat of his brow until the day of his death. Finally, their Creator banished them from Eden, their beautiful home, sentencing them to laborious lives. He also set up well armed security to ensure they would never return. The couple's action had far reaching effects, and we are told that their actions had a negative effect on every human after that.

THE PROMISE OF CHANGE AND TRIUMPH

Despite their banishment and the consequences of their disobedience, their Creator still showed love and care. He provided clothing for them and offered them hope. He promised them that one day the child of the woman would deliver them and crush the serpent that had deceived them. This was a promise of ultimate triumph over their enemy.

HUMANKIND'S WIRING

The Genesis Blueprint reveals the following attributes about us as humans, some of which make us different from other living things:

- *Creatures of Great Value and Worth:* The first humans—unlike the animals or plants—were made in the image and likeness of their Creator. This gave them a unique identity. The Designer placed his distinct logo on them in making them like himself. This of course is a great compliment and speaks of our worth, value and power. We too are designers and creators.

- *Wired for Spiritual and Physical Relationships:* Although the man had a relationship with his Creator who would often meet with him, his Creator saw that it was not good for the man to be alone. The man needed another of his kind to help him fulfil the purpose for which he was created. Therefore, He created a woman for man. The man was given a fitting partner to help him accomplish his purpose. Relationships are vital to our success. We need fitting relationships to win (both divine and human).

- *Created with a Purpose for a Purpose: The purpose of humans* was stated before their creation—Trustees of the Designer's estate, rulers of the earth, air, land and sea; commissioned to be fruitful, to multiply and expand, and to guard and care for where they lived. We, too, have a unique purpose within this broad purpose for humankind. This book will help you to discover that unique purpose. **Note well:** The directive given to the couple is the shared purpose we have with the rest of humankind. We also have an individual specific role (purpose) on this planet called Earth. Our shared purpose requires us to manage the resources around us and to help humankind.

- *Created to be Productive and Successful:* The first command given to humankind as well as the other living things was to be fruitful and multiply. This speaks of effectiveness and productivity. We are not just here to eat, drink and be merry. There is work to do! We are not meant to be idle. The first thing the creator did was to bless the living ones he made. The term "bless" means empowered to prosper. We are created to prosper, to win.

- *Creatures Wired for Work and Rest:* We are unique creatures who must work but also in need of rest. Working and resting are part of design to win at life. The man was given the task to work the ground and to guard and care for it. This was his environment—his home, a garden called Eden. There was no pay involved, and he was not working for provision but according to purpose and pleasure. The work at that point was not arduous or painful. I believe when we do work, we love; we find fulfillment in working. We also see in the story that the Great Designer paused to rest during the creation process. I believe this is prescriptive and instructive to us. We need to have a good work-rest ratio, if we are to win at life.

- *Creatures in Need of a Home and Resources to Live:* The humans were surrounded by a beautiful environment with all they needed for life and work. Food was in abundance; they had a home, and they lacked nothing. There was no poverty. They were not struggling to put food on their table or to take care of themselves. The lack of resources is an obstacle to overcome in order to win at life.

- *Creatures with the Prospect of a Long Healthy Life:* They were not expected to die. There was no pain or disease. Therefore, we too should try to live as healthily as possible and strive to eradicate disease.

- *Creatures of Accountability:* There was a rule or boundary set up to protect the couple, and as long as they obeyed that rule, all was well. They were held accountable for breaking the rule. If we are to win at life, we need to establish boundaries and systems of both personal and societal accountability or else there will be anarchy. We also need to protect the vulnerable

with the establishment of rules of law and order. Additionally, we must remember that there
is One to whom we all will have to one day give
an account for how we live our lives.

While the Genesis blueprint reveals the general
qualities of humankind, there is an individual
uniqueness which is not to be found in the Genesis
blueprint. It has to do with your family, genetics,
cultural heritage, talents, gifts, life experiences and
your beliefs and concerns developed along your
journey of life. These things make you uniquely
YOU and different from every other human being.
After all, no one else has your fingerprint or eyes.
Those things are uniquely yours and the clues to
your unique mission and purpose here on earth.
Career development helps you to recognize your
uniqueness.

EFFECTIVE DESIGNING

The Genesis blueprint reveals our unique creative
potential as creatures made in the image of a Great
Designer. We too are designers and, to be an effective designer, it would be wise to follow the pattern
of the Great Designer who made the universe. Here
now are six (6) patterns of a successful designer
which you should personalize:

- *Being Intentional and Strategic:* This is seen in
  the orderliness of the Great Designer's creative
  work. Some things are only put into place after
  other things are made. For example, the first humans are made after the natural environment
  has been prepared for them. The trees which
  were created first serve as food for the humans

after they are created. The Great Designer assigns purpose and roles to that which He creates. In this same way, in planning for our success, we too should be intentional and strategic and understand our purpose and role in life.

- *Planning and Execution:* The decision, "let us make a new creation –humanity," is followed by the making of humanity. To plan without acting is futile. Effective designers plan first and then execute their plans.

- *Building in Stages:* Understand that your design will not come into being all at once. The design project took six days. This reminds us that success does not come overnight, and we need to be patient.

- *Planning for Eventualities:* The designer had a plan to deal with the failure of the humans—the seed of the woman will eventually settle the score. Effective designers plan for eventualities.

- *Collaborating to Get Things Done:* The statement "let us" indicates collaboration and reminds us that no one succeeds alone. You need support to achieve your goals and dreams.

- *Evaluating Your Work:* At the end of each day of creation, the Great Designer appraised his work and said it was good. In the same way, a successful life designer should evaluate his work to see if it is good, and should build things that he can be proud of. A successful designer is pleased with his work.

As you *Design to Win*, bear these patterns in mind and adopt them. Follow suit and use these patterns to be the "Deputy Architect" of your life. You are the Deputy, because God, the Great Designer, is Chief, and He knows what He desires for your life. It's best to align your plans with His, or your plans may be ultimately thwarted and end in futility.

DESIGN TO WIN ACTIVITY

Read Genesis 1-3 and answer the following questions:

a) List 1 to 3 other qualities/characteristics of a successful life designer that you want to adopt from the Genesis 1-3 blueprint that were not previously mentioned.

b) Write your answers to these five existential questions?

- *Who am I? – Identity*
- *Where am I from? – Origin*
- *Where am I going? – Destination*
- *What am I here to do? – Contribution*
- *Why am I here? – Purpose*

CHAPTER 8:
DISCOVERING YOURSELF

*"The best work, the best career, for you,
the one that makes you happiest and
most fulfilled, is going to be the one
that uses: your favourite transferable
skills, in your favourite subjects, fields
or special knowledges, in a job that
offers you your preferred people
environments, your preferred working
conditions, with your preferred salary
or other rewards, working towards
your preferred goals and values."*
—Dick Bolles

Two of the ways of choosing or changing careers are: a self-inventory and use of career tests/instruments. I've designed a special self-inventory survey, "The Design to Win Survey," to help you to analyze your life and make decisions about your future. The survey is included in this chapter. In terms of the career and personality tests, I have provided the links to these free tools, which you can use to discover your personality type and career possibilities. There is also a link to a strength finder test which will be useful to you. I encourage you to take the time to do all the activities, even though it will be a little time-consuming. As a Jamaican proverb says, "if you want good, your nose afi run," which means anything of substance will cause some discomfort and require hard work. The aim is to help you to make decisions about who you are, to recognize where you are now and determine where you would like to go.

A WORD TO CAREER STARTERS
[AGES 16-24]

It was the final year of high school, and I was excited about my future possibilities. My mom had promised that if I passed all my CXC subjects that she would "cream" my hair. In Jamaica, creaming refers to the process of straightening ones hair. Well lo and behold, I passed all my subjects, but the promise was not met. Even more, I wanted to go to Sixth Form like the rest of my friends, but she had other plans. I wanted to be a chemist, but she wanted to send me to Teachers' College, which in hindsight was a continuation of the legacy of teaching on my paternal side of the family. My grandmother, grandaunt, father and an uncle had all been teachers. I however, resented this.

Consequently, this was a most miserable time of my life. I felt I was too brilliant for teaching, and only those who did not perform well in high school chose that career. Oh how wrong I was! Nevertheless, my misery continued throughout my time in teachers' college from the age of 17-20. During the first week of college, I had an accident and damaged my back. Then I began my rebellion against my mom. However, the die was cast and I could not change my career trajectory at that time.

I remember on teaching practice, my internal invigilator complimented me. She said I would be a good teacher. Over the years I remembered her remarks. Additionally, a friend at church said, much to my dismay, that God had called me to teach. Fast forward twenty years later. While teaching Career Guidance at a vocational training institute, I realized that the best part of my day was teaching the trainees. I came alive whenever I went to teach them. The trainees enjoyed my classes immensely, and similarly to my internal assessor's observation, my colleagues and even the managers have all said the same, "You are gifted at teaching. You seem to love what you do. You are a good teacher."

The truth now is that I have come to love teaching but not traditional subjects. In college, I was trained to teach General Science and Spanish. After undergraduate and graduate studies, I taught theological courses and Spanish related subjects. However, those never gave me joy like teaching life skills and how to make effective career and life choices. I now recognize that career development, which involves teaching, is the perfect field to utilize the gift of teaching and fulfil the call to empower youths to win at life.

Why did I tell this story? Many young people in their beginning years are forced by parents to make career choices that are not their own. This often results in misery for the child. In my case, thankfully, it has worked out. I realize in hindsight that my mother could not afford to send me to university, and what she was trying to do was to position me to take care of myself from early on.

Unfortunately, this was not clearly communicated to me. As an adult, now I understand, but I did not back then. When there are financial constraints, this

sometimes is a necessary choice. The interim training and work can serve as a stepping stone to later
doing what you really love. If you are a young person whose parents have financial constraints, I
would encourage you to find a stepping stone field
of interest to serve as a platform to later pursue
your ideal career. However, do some research before to see if there are scholarship opportunities,
financial aid or alternative ways to pursue your
ideal career/profession from the start. Do not leave
it all up to your parents.

Furthermore, if your parents can afford it, but are
insisting on you doing what they want, I recommend having your guidance counsellor, a teacher,
relative or someone your parents respect talk to
your parents on your behalf. But before you do this,
do a self-inventory to find out what you really want.
Investigate thoroughly your preferred career and
the path to getting there. Create a plan on paper.
I'm sure this kind of thinking and action will im-
press your parents, and hopefully they will comply.
If this still does not work, you may have to do what
they tell you, since you cannot afford to further develop yourself on your own and may be under age.

If presenting your plan does not work, do what
they ask as a stepping stone and later pursue your
ideal life and career when you are of age. In some
cases, perhaps like me, you may find out that your
parents were right after all. They may see a gift in
you that you are not seeing in yourself now.
Whatever the outcome, find a legitimate way to use
your gift to create impact and income and pursue
your ideal life and career.

Know this assuredly, that doing work you love is
vital to your health. You cannot do effective work
for long in doing what you hate. Don't make your

working years miserable. Perhaps this is one reason why people are now changing careers almost every five years. I want you to get it right early.

A WORD TO CAREER REDESIGNERS [AGES 25-34]

Are you merely working for survival rather than significance? Are you struggling to make ends meet while you work? Are you miserable with your current job? If so, there is hope. When I was 25 years old, I was miserable with my job. I dreaded going to the classroom to teach the students. Given my friendly disposition, youth and inexperience, it was difficult to exercise proper classroom control. Things were further compounded because I was teaching students in a community prone to violence. The students had significant behavioural challenges. This partly led to my resignation, although I did feel a call to missionary work at that time.

After resigning, my principal invited me to return for six months in order to find a replacement for my position. Well, this request gave me nightmares. In one nightmare, students were throwing chairs at me, and I was greatly distressed. I knew my time in the classroom at this level was coming to a close although I had to return to it for a while. I survived the six months and finished my time well. The school even gave me a plaque of appreciation for my invaluable service. The problems at the time unleashed my ingenuity, and I created various initiatives to empower the students and maintain classroom control. However, I did not plan properly for my next step, and for two years I struggled financially, emotionally and otherwise.

The reason I am sharing this story is that every transition should be properly planned. Unless fired, do not just leave your job like that. While you are working try to save 3-6 months of living expenses or have an emergency fund. Simplify your lifestyle. Another alternative is to see if you can find another job or study part time while you work. There are many who make their transition slowly in this manner. Do a self-inventory and find out your preferred career path and how to get there. Do informational interviews with persons who are doing what you want to do. Investigate thoroughly and make a plan. As much as possible, transition slowly and carefully, especially when children are involved.

If you are more on the adventurous side, take the jump but consider the consequences carefully. The redesign process usually takes 3-5 years and it is often painful. There will be obstacles, including people who think you are crazy. Don't do it alone, if you don't have to. Do self-development courses, workshops or seminars. Use the internet to educate yourself as much as possible. Join online groups and network with those in your field of interest. Ask them how they did it. Study the people who are successful in your field of interest. Get a mentor if possible. This is one of the fastest way to successfully redesign your life.

There is a movement called *Live Your Legend*, founded by Scott Dinsmore, that has some useful tools to help people who want to do work they love. They have an online site and free resources to help. There is also a readiness to change free test that they do which I would advise you to take to really confirm your readiness for change. Visit https://liveyourlegend.net/ for more information.

Another great organization that can help you with career transition and redesigning your life is BestWork Inc., which has been successfully helping persons for over 50 years with their trademark proven Life/Work Design process. Visit http://bestworkinc.com/ for more information.

Speak to others who have travelled this route successfully. Speak to a career or life coach for further guidance but don't make the decision in isolation and without counting the cost. Schedule a session through our Design to Win academy for clarity, direction and guidance. There is safety and wisdom in the multitude of counsel.

SUCCESS MODELS

During my times of redesigning my life and career transitions, which I have done at least three times, having models of success was vital. Reading their stories inspired and motivated me to continue my journey. This strategic key of having success models has transformed my life. In moments of despair, the stories of others provide the motivation and inspiration you need to continue your journey. As previously said, success is not achieved overnight. It can be long and laborious, and there will be many obstacles to overcome along the way. In your head, you have to fight "Mr. Defeat," as Dr. David Schwartz reminds us in his book *The Magic of Thinking Big*. Mr. Defeat will tell you all the reasons why you cannot do x, y or z.

Many of us have all kinds of excuses and reasons why we cannot achieve our God-given goals and dreams. We are suffering from the disease Dr. Schwartz labels as "excusistis"–

- I'm too old;
- I'm too young;
- I'm not smart enough;
- it's too late;
- I'm not healthy;
- I'm from the wrong side of town;
- I've been rejected too many times; etc.

Yet we can all find successful persons who triumphed over all excuses. This is why studying success models is so important. Their stories remind us, that if they did it, so can we!

I usually have my students do group presentations on success models, but you can do it as a personal exercise, if you are reading this book for individual use. Here is what you can do. Identify 1-3 success models under 30 and over 40; that is, persons who achieved significant success in their field of endeavour by age 30, and those who did it after age 40. These could be persons you know personally or are international icons. They could be your national heroes, sports figures, political figures or someone doing well in a field/career of your interest. In your research look for the following:

- Brief biography (age, family, education, etc.)
- Accomplishments of the person
- Obstacles they had to overcome
- Philosophy, habits and or attitudes that led to their success
- 1-3 keys to their success that you would like to adopt
- Any other important point

Take note of your findings.

DESIGN TO WIN ACTIVITIES
CAREER AND PERSONALITY TESTS

Visit the links provided to do the Kiersey Temperament Sorter Test, Holland's Code Career Test and the Strength Finder Test. An alternative to the Holland's code is Richard Bolles's Party Exercise which can be done in less than 5 minutes. If you have a copy of *What Colour is Your Parachute?* (2018), it's included on pages 132-133. You can also simply Google all these tests: *Holland's Code Career Test, The Party Exercise/ Holland Party Game, Kiersey Temperament Test and The Strength Finder Aptitude Test.*

Holland's Career Code Test, https://www.truity-
.com/test/holland-code-career-test/
Kiersey Temperament Sorter, https://www.keirsey-
.com/sorter/register.aspx
Strength Finder Aptitude Test, http://richardstep-
.com/richardstep-strengths-weaknesses-
aptitude-test/free-aptitude-test-find-your-
strengths-weaknesses-online-version/

Upon completion of these tests, answer the following questions:

a) Identify your personality type and record a brief description of the same.
b) Note three of your strengths and weaknesses.
c) Identify at least 10 career/occupational options or interests.
d) Type in your 3-letter Holland code using O*NET or visit Holland's Code Occupation Database–VISTa Life/Career Cards

(http://www.vista-cards.com/occupations/) to get more information concerning your career/ occupational interests. Then click on the occupations of interest to see what tasks, skills, knowledge, abilities, work context and education are required for those occupations.

A LIFE-ANALYSIS

It's time to do your *Design to Win* Survey to learn more about your uniqueness, present condition and future desires for your life and career. The Design to Win survey has been created to help with this process. The survey is intentionally invasive and intensive. For things to change, one has to do a rigorous life-analysis. The survey can be completed in 30-45 minutes. However, if you are a Career Redesigner, it will take about an hour because you will be required to complete both Sections A and B. If doing the Design to Win Fundamentals course, submit your answers to your instructor/coach. It would be wise to set up a coaching or consultation session to discuss the results and the way forward. See the survey on the next page.

THE DESIGN TO WIN SURVEY

Answer all questions. This is a life analysis which is part of the Discovery process to help you plan the way forward and to identify areas for personal coaching or improvement.

SECTION A

1. Do you find yourself constantly dwelling on past successes or failures?
   [ ] Yes   [ ] No

2. Do you learn something valuable from all mistakes?
   [ ] Yes   [ ] No

3. Does life seem futile and the future hopeless to you?
   [ ] Yes   [ ] No

4. Do you have a plan for your life for the next 5 years?
   [ ] Yes   [ ] No

   —Is this plan in writing?
   [ ] Yes   [ ] No

5. Do you consider your mind a resource?
   [ ] Yes   [ ] No

6. Do you have a habit of saving?
   [ ] Yes   [ ] No

—If yes, do you have 1-3 months' salary/lunch
   money saved?
[ ] Yes   [ ] No

7. Do you suffer from any of these fears?

- Fear of poverty
  [ ] Yes   [ ] No
- Fear of criticism
  [ ] Yes   [ ] No
- Fear of ill health
  [ ] Yes   [ ] No
- Fear of loss of love of someone
  [ ] Yes   [ ] No
- Fear of old age
  [ ] Yes   [ ] No
- Fear of death
  [ ] Yes   [ ] No
- Fear of failure
  [ ] Yes   [ ] No
- Fear of rejection
  [ ] Yes   [ ] No
- Other

  _____

  _____

8. Do you believe you were created for a special
   purpose?
[ ] Yes   [ ] No
—If yes, what is that purpose?

   _____

   _____

9. Do you believe in life after death?
   [ ] Yes   [ ] No
   —Explain your answer.

   _____

   _____

   _____

10. Do you know or have ideas about the
    contribution you would like to make to society
    before you die?
    [ ] Yes   [ ] No
    —If yes, describe briefly or list them.

    _____

    _____

    _____

11. Name 3 of your strengths or things you are really
    good at.

    _____

    _____

    _____

12. Name 3 of your most damaging weaknesses and what are you doing to correct them.

_____

_____

_____

13. Reflect on and review the last 5-10 years of your life. If you are older than 20 years, review the last 10 years. If you are under twenty, review the last 5 years by answering the questions below. As you review and answer the questions below, bear in mind the following areas to guide your answers: material and financial; spiritual, mental and emotional; career and education; relationships; health and recreation; and service and contribution.

a) What have you accomplished in the last 10 years of your life? List 5-10 things.

_____

_____

_____

_____

_____

b) What could you have accomplished that you
    have not? List 3-5 things.

_____

_____

_____

c) What do you wish you had accomplished?
    List 1-3 things.

_____

_____

d) Why didn't you accomplish them? List 1-3
    reasons.

_____

_____

_____

14. If enough money was not an obstacle, describe
    what your ideal life and career/work would look
    like? For example: Where would you go? What
    would you like to have, own, see or do? List as
    many things as possible.

_____

_____

15. List 1-3 things which you feel are or have been obstacles to your progress. These include significant habits, attitudes, heartaches and patterns which have been holding you back.

_____

_____

_____

16. How would you describe your relationship with these persons? Use the terms *satisfactory, excellent, poor, undecided, non-existent, not applicable* to describe each:

   • Your parents (deceased or alive)

   _____

   • Friends (Past and present)

   _____

   • Siblings and other relatives

   _____

   • Schoolmates

   _____

   • Work colleagues

   _____

- Spouse/partner

  _____

- Children

  _____

18. Who among your acquaintances, associates, friends or family:

   - Encourages you the most?

     _____

   - Cautions you the most?

     _____

   - Discourages you the most?

     _____

19. How much of your time out of every 24 hours do you devote to:

   - Occupation/school work _____
   - Sleep _____
   - Play/relaxation/socializing _____
   - Acquiring useful knowledge _____
   - Plain waste _____

20. What do you think about the idea of becoming rich?

_____

_____

_____

21. What connection, if any, do you see between the people with whom you associate most closely and any unhappiness you have been experiencing?

_____

_____

_____

_____

TRUE LIFE-WINNER TEST

Using Zig Ziglar's Test, on a scale of 1-5, with five being the highest, how would you rate yourself in these 8 areas:

Career: doing well in a chosen field   _____

Attitude: freedom from fear and worry—positive mental attitude

    _____

Spiritual: peace with God and peace of mind   _____

Finances: reasonably stable/prosperous and secure

    _____

Relationships: happy and healthy relationships with friends and family

    _____

Personal: achieving set goals   _____

Health: physical and emotional health   _____

Hope (for the future)   _____

SECTION B

CAREER REDESIGNERS ONLY
THOSE WHO ARE IN THE WORKING WORLD

1. If you had to live your life all over again, what are the things you would not get into again? Think of your work, family, friends, community, spiritual life, etc. and list 5 -10 things.

_____

_____

_____

_____

2. If you could not do your present job anymore, but you received 10 million US dollars and never had to work again, what would you spend your time volunteering to do?

_____

_____

3. What are the fields that you most enjoy exploring in magazines, books, seminars, workshop, the internet and life in general?

_____

_____

4. What experiences have you had thus far in life that turned you on and in which you felt you did well? List or describe 3-5 of these.

_____

_____

_____

a) What are the skills that you most enjoyed using in those experiences? List 3-5.

_____

_____

_____

b) If you had to put those skills in an order of preference, which is the skill that you most enjoy using?

_____

c) Is its focus on [   ] data (information), [   ] people or [   ] things? Check one.

5. If you had to visit different work settings in order to learn more about them, which ones would you most likely visit? List 3-5.

_____

_____

_____

6. How could you plan to have more leisure time or more time with loved ones and friends in the present rather than waiting for retirement?

_____

_____

_____

7. What would be your preferred monthly salary range from lowest to highest?

_____ : _____

CHAPTER 9:
WHAT'S YOUR PURPOSE IN LIFE?

*"True leaders are born when you find
something to die for..."*
—Myles Munroe

We are now in Step 2 of the *Design to Win* process: **Decision-Making.** The first major decision we should make is to recognize and pursue our purpose in life. As Napoleon Hill reminds us, "all successful persons have a chief definite aim in life."

THE PURPLE CLOTH AND PURPOSE

At a recent conference, a young man saw me with a purple cloth and then asked, "Miss, are you the lady who presented at my school?" On hearing the name of the school, I said, "yes," and his face "lit up." He said, "I remember you. I was one of the students who held the purple cloth." It was a very memorable and pleasing moment for me, because the purple cloth was now being recognized as part of my brand.

In April 2015, the colour purple became a significant colour in my life, and God has been using a purple cloth to teach me about my worth and value. My middle name, Ionie, means "violet flower," and violet is a form of purple. Purple, due to the history of its making, has often been a symbol of royalty and worth in European cultures. Only people of great financial standing could afford purple cloth and, at one stage, Emperor Nero of Rome made it illegal for the common man to wear purple cloth. The story of my purple cloth, has been a vital part of my understanding of the importance of knowing one's purpose and how to overcome life's hurdles.

In August 2014, I ended my commitment with Operation Mobilization as a full-time missionary. During the first year of my service, I decorated the Board Room for a function and never removed the decorative material. The decorative material included strips of purple cloth and, shortly before leaving the organization, I removed most of the decor and returned the materials to the owner. I was accidentally left with a piece of purple cloth. I then used this cloth to wrap the pot of the potted plant that remained in the office.

When I left the organization, I saw no further use for the purple cloth. I took it home and placed it at the bottom of my laundry basket for almost nine months. I am not sure why it did not end up in the garbage basket, but now I am glad it did not. You see, one of my friends was getting married and mine was the honor of being the Maid of honor. One of the duties as maid of honour is to throw a bridal shower, and it was then that the purple cloth became significant again. I needed material for the décor of the bridal shower venue and I remembered the purple cloth. I washed it and used it as part of décor.

Surprisingly, this was not the end of the purple cloth. It began to "speak" to me and teach me some significant life lessons. I began to realize some amazing ways that I could retool it and use it in my presentations. When I shared these insights in presentations, whether preaching, teaching or doing a motivational talk, I began receiving standing ovations and applauses. The purple cloth has travelled beyond Jamaica and has been used to teach life-changing lessons as far away as Uganda and South Africa.

Imagine that! That which was once at the bottom of the pile of a dirty clothes laundry basket has made it not only to the top of the pile, but out of the pile and is being used for significant impact to change lives. And all of this began with a renewed vision of purpose. When you don't know your purpose, you may often be misused, abused and in some cases discarded. Your life may become useless, and you end up wasting your years and the precious gift of life.

Regardless of the topic of my presentation, the purple cloth consistently enlightens my audience on the need for self-worth and an understanding of their purpose. The major lesson here is that, if you don't recognize your purpose and the possible uses of your life, you too will remain at the bottom of the pile. On the other hand, when you do recognize your purpose, many doors will open for you and take you—like the purple cloth—to places you never dared to dream of going.

THE IMPORTANCE OF PURPOSE

Every design is built for a purpose, and every architect has a purpose for his plan. In the same way, your Great Designer had a purpose in mind for you when he created you. That purpose is your reason to travel on planet Earth. One of the questions Immigration officers love to ask is: "what is your reason/purpose for travel?" Failure to answer this question properly may prevent you from getting to your destination, and so it is in life. Failure to answer this question may mean failure to fulfil your destiny, being left at the bottom of the pile or a complete failure in life. This is an issue with which many people struggle, but all successful persons know their purpose.

My definition of success has to do with purpose. Here is my simple definition of success. **It is the fulfillment of purpose.** Any object or thing whether living or inanimate that fails to fulfil its purpose and function is worthy of being deemed a failure. Let me take that definition one step further. "Success is fulfilling your God-given purpose. It is bringing to life that which you were designed to do and doing it well, that is, with excellence." Another simple definition of success is Earle Nightingale's definition: "the progressive realization of a worthy ideal."

Now, let's get back to purpose. According to multi-best-selling author and leadership expert, the late Dr. Myles Munroe, "Purpose is when you know and understand what you were born to accomplish." Munroe was famous for saying that, "the greatest tragedy in life is not death but a life lived without purpose." Another leadership expert, Dr. John Maxwell has said in several of his presentations that the two most important days of your life are "the day when you were born and the day you discover why." What profound statements on purpose! When you discover why you were born, it is then that you really start living with purpose.

Knowing your purpose will benefit you in at least seven ways. You will:

1. Become successful or achieve more in life
2. Use your time more efficiently
3. Focus better and give attention to things that really matter
4. Follow your dreams instead of the dreams of others
5. Gain courage and strength in the face of adversity
6. Have a reason to live and add significance and length to your life
7. Improve your decision-making

The benefits of purpose according to Richard Leider, author of the *Power of Purpose*, who has spent over three decades studying purpose, include health, happiness, healing and longevity. He notes that even studies done on patients with dementia show that they do better when they have a sense of purpose.

FINDING MY PURPOSE

Leider notes that the path to finding purpose is not as complicated as we often make it. He says purpose is in essence a combination of your gifts, passions and values. I agree with Leider on his postulation of purpose. I believe purpose is connected with service/contribution. It is a mix of your gifts and passions and how you would want to use those for the glory of God and the good of humanity. Purpose also entails doing what you love and not just what you are good at. It is recognized or activated when you are engaged in something that causes you to easily lose of track of time.

Furthermore, purpose is connected with your vocation. The word vocation/calling is another way to speak of your mission in life. Mission, when used in respect to our life and work, says Richard Bolles, has always been a religious concept from beginning to end. To have a mission or destiny, vocation or calling implies, "Someone who calls... Someone who determined the destination for us" (2018, 278). Our purpose is also our chief mission in life, and this inevitably lands us in the "lap of God." This factor is often missing from our conversations where a belief in God is seen as ludicrous.

In this regard, I love what Bolles says about our chief mission (purpose) in life which is three-fold. First of all, it is a shared mission "to seek to stand hour by hour in the conscious presence of God, the One from whom your mission is derived." Secondly, it is "to do what you can, moment by moment, day by day, step by step to make this world a better place, following the leading and guidance of God's Spirit within and around you." Thirdly, it is something that is uniquely yours, "to exercise the Talent that you particularly came to earth to use your greatest gift, which you delight to use, in the place(s) or setting (s) that God has caused to appeal to you the most, and for the purposes that God most needs to have done in the world" (2018, 280).

If we bear these concepts in mind as delineated by Bolles and Leider, we can begin to discover our unique purpose. Both men simplify the recognition of this purpose as the engagement of a Talent which when exercised gives you the greatest pleasure. To reiterate, it is usually the one that, when you use it, causes you to lose all sense of time. I know when I am walking in purpose. I feel a deep sense of satisfaction when I am engaged in certain activities. I come alive! I ooze with life when doing it!

That's how I know when I am walking in purpose. I have come to realize that the understanding of purpose is usually a journey over time, and I have found three methods of discovering your purpose in life. In my case, all three methods helped me to recognize my purpose along with prayer.

a) *Divine Revelation:* This can be supernaturally revealed. Famous biblical examples include John the Baptist, Jesus of Nazareth, Sampson, Abraham and the Apostle Paul. In the case of Jesus, John and Sampson, an angel appeared to their parents to convey the purpose of the child. In Abraham's case, he had an encounter with God, and in Paul's case, it was similar and a prophet named Ananias confirmed it. Sometimes it is a vision or dream or just a strong impression in your heart or, God may send someone to tell you, as in my case and that of the Apostle Paul.

b) *Reflection/Introspection/Self-questioning:* This is pretty much asking yourself strategic questions about your passion, gifts, experiences, major concerns and the difference you would like to make in the world. It includes reflecting on your life and what matters most to you or where you were happiest or saddest and making a decision to do something about it.

c) *Feedback from Others:* Sometimes others will see in you what you cannot see in yourself. This entails suggestions from individuals about what you are really good at and persons pointing out the attributes and natural tendencies they observe about you. You can also use feedback to confirm the desires in your heart. Make note of what they say and be willing to try it.

3 Methods of Discovering Purpose

Divine Revelation
Pray and ask for Divine revelation.

Reflection/Introspection/ Self-questioning
Time in solitude asking strategic questions re passion, gifts, experiences, major concerns etc.

Feedback from Others
What are others saying to you?

Important Reminders—remember these four things regarding purpose:

a) Your purpose is connected with **service, use** and **contribution** to others. It is not just what you want for yourself. How you serve and define that contribution will be based on your gifts, passion and beliefs/values.

b) Clarifying your purpose takes time and is often discovered by trial and error.

c) Your purpose statements may change over time, and that's okay. What matters is finding a compelling why for living and acting in accordance with it, so that you do not merely exist in life.

d) Remember the purple cloth! As long as I could not see its purpose, it was discarded and inactive at the bottom of the pile. If you want to progress, you've got to get a hold of your purpose.

DESIGN TO WIN ACTIVITIES

Writing Purpose Statements and Taglines:

1. Write a long purpose statement. The long statement may include your gifts or talents, methods, target group and location.

2. Write a tagline or a short statement.

See guiding scenarios, questions and examples provided to assist you. If you are a person of faith, make sure you pray for a revelation regarding your purpose.

PURPOSE GUIDING SCENARIOS

A) Imagine you will be interviewed on Oprah or any popular television programme. What would they say to introduce you in 30 seconds which basically sums up what your life and career is about? What would be your claim to fame?

B) Find a nice quiet place, grab a sheet of paper and use this pool of 21 questions to guide you. One of the blockages to finding purpose is technology and busyness. You have to block out distractions to hear your heart and recognize your purpose. Answer as many questions as you feel are necessary. Your answers are clues to your purpose; examine them. Are big concepts emerging? Are there recurring ideas or things? Note these! These are big clues if not answers to your purpose. *Try to capture or summarize your answers in a paragraph and then later a statement.*

Purpose Discovery Questions

1. What is my chief definite aim in life?
2. What are the uses of my life?
3. What talents and gifts do I possess?
4. How could my talents and gifts be used to serve others in an amazing way?
5. What problems do I feel called to solve?
6. What irritates me or makes me sad?
7. What makes me happy or causes me to smile?
8. What is it that I see in life that I feel I could improve or change?
9. What difference do I wish to make in the world?
10. What ideas do I have that will not go away?
11. What legacy do I want to leave for my family or country?
12. What is the most important goal that I want to achieve in life?
13. What mark do I want to leave in this world after I die?
14. What does God want me to do with my life?
15. What is the greatest service I feel I could make to mankind?
16. What is it that when I do it, I feel most alive, satisfied, confident or fulfilled?
17. What work would I love to do even if I were not paid for?
18. What one thing do I want to be known for when others call my name?
19. What burning problem(s) would I like to fix?

20. What life issue causes me the greatest pain?
21. With what do others most identify me?

Long Statement Examples:

- I empower people around the world to win at life through education, writing and speaking.
- To serve as a leader, live a balanced life, and apply ethical principles to make a significant difference.
- To be a teacher and to be known for inspiring my students to be more than they thought they could be.
- To use my gifts of intelligence, charisma and serial optimism to cultivate the self-worth and net-worth of women around the world.

Short Statement Examples and Taglines:

- To inspire people to live healthier lives. Tagline: *inspiration and health.*
- To exalt God and empower people to win at life. Tagline: *Exalt God... Empower People.*
- I help people to win at work and succeed at life. Tagline: *win at work... succeed at life.*
- I help people to live vibrant lives. Tagline: *Vibrant Living.*
- To inspire people through art. Tagline: *Art is life.*

CHAPTER 10: CHOOSING YOUR DESTINATION

YOUR IDEAL LIFE AND CAREER VISION

We are still in Step 2 of the Design to Win process (**Decision-Making**). To reiterate, all designers or creators begin with a vision of their end product. They know the purpose behind the creation of that product, and so it should be with our lives. As you progress in creating your Design to Win, you must have a vision of your ideal destination in life. What does a winning life and career look like for you? Your 1-5 year progress plan must be a subset of this larger life-vision. Your accomplishments in these years must be stops along the way to eventually get to that ultimate destination. Thinking and acting this way will ensure you live a purpose driven life. It is also the way to "astonish the world," as Bolles has said, because you will know where you are going and what you want to do with your life.

We will do as Stephen Covey, author of *The 7 Habits of Highly Effective People,* says: "Begin with the end in mind," then work backwards. Like an architect, you too must see the entire house, create a blueprint to build it and then build it, block upon block, until it is finished. And remember, a true life-winner thinks of earthly and eternal destination points.

In this decision-making phase of the *Design to Win* process, bear in mind the travel analogy. Think of going to a travel agent and how s/he will work with you to get to your intended destination. Generally speaking, the process utilizes the following four things:

1. Identification of the intended final destination, time-frame and reason (s) for travel—Decision-making [step 2]

2. Selecting the best route—Designing [step 3]

3. Gathering the necessary resources and preparing to travel—Development [step 4]

4. Travelling—Doing it [step 5]

The subject matter of this chapter is the identification of your intended final destination.

DESIGN TO WIN ACTIVITY

Choose one of the three options provided to decide your ideal life and career destination. When you choose your option, write it in the past tense, because the idea is capturing the end, which means you already did these things. You can make a list or write a nice paragraph or two. I also encourage you to find sample tributes, obituaries or short citations to guide you in preparing to write yours. These can be found online or via a local newspaper.

Option 1: The End of Your Life—Eulogy / Obituary / Death Tribute

The eulogy idea has been used by various personal development professionals. However, authors Michael Hyatt and Daniel Harkavy captured it well and developed the concept in their book *Living Forward*. This would be an excellent book to read. I have tweaked the method somewhat.

1. Fast forward to the end of your life, imagine it's your funeral or an article is written about you in the newspaper upon your death. What is it that you would want them to say about you, in no more than 250 words? In your description, be as concise and specific as possible about the things that would really matter to you or you would really want to be remembered for above everything else.

2. Let your description be holistic by bearing in mind the seven (7) areas of the wellness wheel as a guide: career and business, relationships (family and friends), education/intellect, spiritual and emotional (personality), financial and social and community contribution.

3. Use these guiding questions to help you create this vision. You do not need to answer them individually.

   • What was your greatest contribution or legacy to community, country or family?
   • What educational or career pursuits did you follow?
   • Did you work or start your own business?

- Did you write anything?
- What were you like with friends and family?
- How many children or grandchildren did you have?
- What did people appreciate most about you?
- What organizations or groups were you part of?
- What about your principles and personality?

Option 2: A Living Tribute at 80 years old

Fast forward to age 80. There is a function being held in your honour, perhaps a birthday party or some honorary function put on by family or colleagues. What would they say about you? Bear in mind the 7 areas of the wellness wheel. Your description should be as concise as possible about the things that would really matter to you, or what you would really want to be remembered for above everything else. Use the same guiding questions to help you.

Option 3: Your Legacy—Citation

Fast forward to age 80 and on a special occasion, you are presented with a citation, no more than 250 words. What would be the content of your citation? Be as concise and specific as possible about the things that really mattered to you and what you accomplished. Describe your defining legacy.

Chapter 11:
Choosing Your Major Life and Career Goals

Before you can score,
you must first have a goal.
—Greek Proverb

This is the final part of the Decision-Making phase of the *Design to Win* process; in this part of the process, you are going to choose the stops along the way, as you journey towards your intended ultimate destination in life. These stops are what we will refer to as goals. We will also look at some reasons and rewards for making these stops. This interim journey is estimated to be 1-5 years, and you will be making key life and career decisions for your future.

Travel Smart Advisory

When it comes to setting and keeping goals, many persons struggle in this area. However, I believe we are all already goal-setters and goal-achievers, but some goals are harder to achieve than others. If you ever travelled from one place to another or kept an appointment, that's proof you are already a goal achiever. You made a decision and acted on it. That was a goal accomplished.

I believe part of the failure to keep big goals is because we do not set goals in writing with definite plans to achieve them. I often cite in an old Harvard Study cited by Mark McCormack in *What They Don't Teach You in the Harvard Business School* (1986) to prove the effectiveness of penning our goals with plans to accomplish them.

In 1979, interviewers asked new graduates from the Harvard MBA Program about their goals and found that:

- 84% had no specific goals at all;
- 13% had goals but they were not committed to paper;
- 3% had clear, written goals and plans to accomplish them.

In 1989, the interviewers again interviewed the graduates of that class. Here are the results 10 years later:

The 13% of the class who had goals were earning, on average, twice as much as the 84% who had no goals at all.

Even more staggering—the 3% who had clear, written goals were earning, on average, ten times as much as the other 97% put together.

Goal-Setting Fears and Frustrations

If using the travel analogy, a goal is really a decision to move from one point to another in the different areas of our lives. However, we often fail to move or complete the journey because of a number of factors including the following:

- *Fear of Travelling*—This is induced by concerns about approval, rejection, past negative experiences and the opinions of others etc.

- *Travel Cost*—The price is too much, too much work, can't afford it, hurdles/obstacles etc.

- *Insufficiency, Ignorance and Inexperience*— We don't know enough to get there and lack the skills and resources to get there.

There are those who take the journey successfully everyday and what has been done already can be done again. It's possible. I offer the following travel smart tips to help you to take the journey and travel well.

Remember the 4Ws:

- *What* and *Where?*—You must decide clearly what you want or where you want to go.

- *Why?*—You must have a strong why for going.

- *When?*—You must be flexible with your time-lines. Expect detours and delays along the way. Sometimes there will be a flight cancellation and you have to abandon that goal but it's part of the process. There will also be some pleasant and unpleasant surprises along the way. This is why in Step 4 of the Design to Win process, we emphasize the development of life management skills and the Art of Life Hurdling.

You will need to develop these skills in order to finish your journey well.

In our *Design to Win* activity, you will be creating holistic goals in the following seven (7) areas of your life for the next 1-5 years:

a) Spiritual Development
b) Financial & Material
c) Career and Business/Profession/Occupation
d) Relationships [Family and Friends]
e) Personal Growth/Self-Improvement and Learning
f) Health & Fitness
g) Social & Community Contribution

DESIGN TO WIN ACTIVITY

Preparation

- Block a time period of at least 30 minutes
- A notepad/sheets of paper/your computer/Ipad etc. and a quiet place
- Pray and dream about the next 1-5 years
- Remember your ultimate destination

Step 1, Option A

- What needs to happen for you to look back and say "these were my best years?"
- If money were no problem, and you could live your ideal life and career, what would you want to be, do, have, achieve, etc. in the 7 areas in the next 1-2 and 3-5 years?

Then list 10 to 12 major things you can think of for the 1-2 year period and do the same for the 3-5 year period. Choose big goals and little goals. They could be related to simple things like vacation, birthday treats, immediate needs and major things like degrees and certifications.

Step 1, Option B:

Use the quick-list 30-second exercise created by success expert Brian Tracy in his book *Reinvention*. As quickly as you can, in 30 seconds or less for each question, write down your answers to the following:

1. What are your three most important business and career goals right now?

   1 _____

   2 _____

   3 _____

2. What are your three most important family and relationship goals right now?

   1 _____

   2 _____

   3 _____

3. What are your three most important health and fitness goals right now?

   1 _____

   2 _____

   3 _____

4. What are your three most important financial goals right now?

   1 _____

   2 _____

   3 _____

5. What are your three most important educational or learning goals right now?

   1 _____

   2 _____

   3 _____

6. What are your three most important social and community goals right now?

   1 _____

   2 _____

   3 _____

7. What are your three most important goals for spiritual development and inner peace right now?

   1 _____

   2 _____

   3 _____

According to Tracy, "when you have only 30 seconds to write down the answers to these questions, your answers will be as accurate as if you had 30 minutes or three hours" (2009, 51-53).

Step 2: Prioritize to Optimize

According to the Pareto principle by Italian economist Vilfredo Pareto, 80% of our results come from 20% input. Your aim in this section is to identify your 20% goals that will give you 80% results. This means you need to find the one stone that can kill two or more birds, and in order to do this, you must narrow down your list of goals.

a) If you chose Step 1, Option A, look back at your 1-2 year and 3-5 year list of goals and narrow down this list in each category to 5 goals respectively and put a special marker to highlight these goals. This means from a list of 20-24 goals that you will end up with five 1-2 year goals and five 3-5 year goals.

—OR—

b) If you chose Step 1, Option B, select the top goal in each category and put a special marker to highlight each of these goals. This means that from a list of 21 goals, you will end up with 7 goals.

Whichever goal setting option you chose, it's time to narrow down these goals even further, because if we chase too many rabbits, we will not catch any.

If you chose Step 1, Option A, at this stage you should have 10 goals in all. Imagine in 24 hours you could be granted 5 of these goals; which five would you choose? Highlight these goals. These are the goals which we will use in creating your life-winning plan to achieve in the Design phase of the

Design to Win process. Of course, in the actual doing phase each year, you will create a list of sub-goals or steps to accomplish these goals each month or each quarter of the year.

If you chose Step 1, Option B, you should have a list of 7 goals at this stage; from this list, narrow down your goals to 5.

These are the 5 most important goals that you should pursue over the next 1-5 years.

Step 4: Personalizing your goals

Rewrite each of these goals in the present tense using "I" statements. I want to you think like a designer and write your goals as finished in your mind. This is a form of expression of faith, seeing the end in mind—the achievement of your goals. Be specific about those goals. Ask yourself: how much and by when? Your goals must also have a timeframe and should include a verb. As the popular acronym says, goals must be Specific, Measurable, Action-Oriented and Time bound (SMART).
For example:

- I save US$1000 by December 2018—instead of "I want more money."
- I am a lawyer by December 2022 —instead of " I want to be a lawyer."
- I read one book each month—instead of "I read more."

Step 5: Reasons and Rewards

Every goal will be tested. Every dream will be attacked and, in moments of frustration, it is your reasons which will keep your goals breathing and enable you to persevere despite the odds. Make a list of five reasons and or five rewards for achieving these goals no matter what. These reasons for example could be:

a) To better my family life
b) To never be hungry again/financial freedom
c) To make my mother proud
d) To leave a legacy
e) To fulfil my purpose and succeed in life

Step 6: Summarizing Your Decisions

Use the Mini Design to Win Blueprint on the next page to capture your decisions in Chapters 9-11. There will be two sections (core values and personal brand) which should be left blank until Chapter 12. Your mini blueprint should be no more than 2 pages and can be placed on a wall or somewhere you can see it often to keep you on track over time.

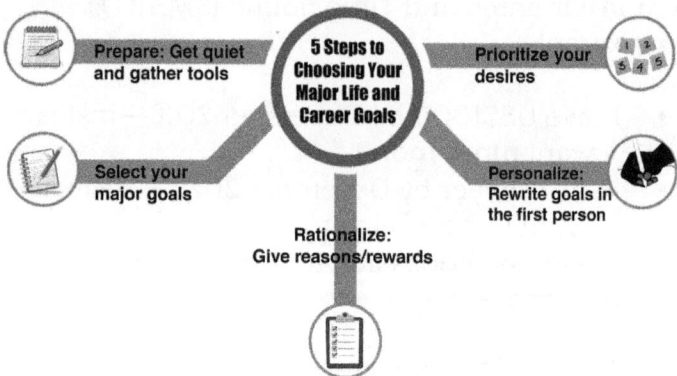

Prepare: Get quiet and gather tools

5 Steps to Choosing Your Major Life and Career Goals

Prioritize your desires

Select your major goals

Personalize: Rewrite goals in the first person

Rationalize: Give reasons/rewards

MINI DESIGN TO WIN BLUEPRINT

Year   20_____ - 20_____

My Life Purpose:

My Ultimate Life and Career Vision:

My Core Values   **My Personal Brand**

1.   1.

2.   2.

3.   3.

4.   4.

5.   5.

My 5 Major Life Goals 20____ to 20____

[Step 2, Option A Results]

1.

2.

3.

4.

5.

OR *[Step 1, Option A Results]*

1-2 Year Goals	3-5 Year Goals
1.	1.
2.	2.
3.	3.
4.	4.
5.	5.

5 Reasons to Accomplish Goals	5 Rewards/Benefits
1.	1.
2.	2.

3.   3.

4.   4.

5.   5.

CHAPTER 12:
YOUR STRATEGIC
PROGRESS PLAN

"To act without planning is fatal.
To have a plan and not act on it
is futile."
—Myles Munroe

In this chapter, you will expand on your Mini Design to Win blueprint to create a detailed action plan to accomplish your major life and career goals over the next 1-5 years. The complete plan has the following elements:

1. Life and Career Vision

2. My Life Purpose

3. My Personal Brand

4. My Core Values

5. My Life and Career Rewards/Reasons

6. My Action Plan

7. Pictures of My Future

WHY CREATE A LIFE AND CAREER PLAN?

Highly effective people are long-term thinkers, goal setters and planners, who pen it to win. Successful people think on paper. Pen it to Win! No architect or designer keeps the sketch in his head. The architect always has a blueprint. Imagine what would happen if you tried to construct a building without one!

In some countries like Jamaica, it is illegal to build without a plan or blueprint approved by the parish council or relevant authority. "Write a vision, and explain on the tables, that he may run who is reading it" (Habakkuk 2:2). We all know that a year from now we are not likely to remember all the details, so pen it to not forget it. Pen it to communicate it. Pen it, so what's in your mind's eye can be brought to light. Pen it to gather resources. Pen it for greater insights and aid. Pen it to seize opportunities. Pen it, lest you give up and forget when there are lengthy delays, detours and disappointments. Pen it, so that the vision will live and not die. Pen it to hold yourself and others accountable.

MY DESIGN TO WIN

In September to December 2014, after leaving full-time missionary service, I took this period to rest, reflect, recharge and reinvent my life. Although, in June of that year I had written down a six page vision of what I believed was God's plan for the next phase of my life, I needed to create an action plan. Part of that action plan included publishing a book each year and establishing myself as a personal development coach and to begin creating impact and income via these avenues. I remember clearly in November 2014 writing down the reason for the steps I was about to make: to exalt God and empower people. The recording of this mission/purpose was more significant than I realized at the time.

It was very difficult to pursue this vision especially in the first year. There were many challenges and times when I felt like giving up. Had it not been for the plan in writing and a strong purpose clearly written, which I revisited numerous times, I would not be reaping the rewards which I am now reaping as I enter year three of my reinvention. New streams of income came in the ways I had envisaged and also in ways I did not plan for, namely, career development.

However, through it all, the purpose remained, and I have had my mini blueprint, on one paper visibly displayed in my bedroom to keep me on track. The point is that your 1-5 year plan must be fluid especially regarding your steps for accomplishment. Don't expect it to all go as planned. Some of my goals had to be painfully laid aside, but new goals and insights emerged which seemed even better than the previous ones. Know this: some goals may change, and that's okay.

What's most important is that you understand your purpose because, though methodologies may change, purpose must remain constant. Keep the original plan to measure your progress year after year. You will find that your plan will also help you to do the following:

- Stay focussed and live a purpose driven-life
- Make better everyday decisions
- Determine which opportunities to seize or not

- To better communicate to others what you are trying to achieve
- Accelerate your progress in life
- Help you to live a life with less regrets

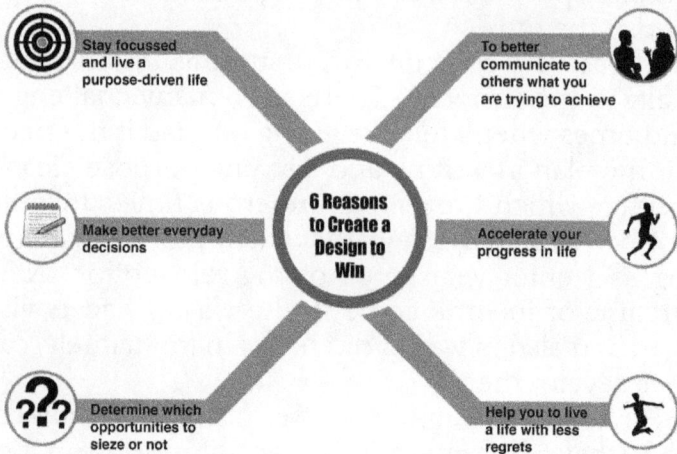

CREATING YOUR CORE VALUES

Core values are your decision-making lens—your right or wrong filter and your internal guidance system on your journey throughout life. In this regard, I find Jamaica's National Pledge an excellent guiding system to select one's core values. The pledge is as follows:

Before God and all mankind, I pledge the love and loyalty of my heart, the wisdom and courage of my mind, the strength and vigour of my body in the service of my fellow citizens; I promise to stand up for Justice, Brotherhood and Peace, to work diligently and creatively, to think generously and honestly, so that Jamaica may, under God, increase in beauty, fellowship and prosperity, and play her part in advancing the welfare of the whole human race.

When I examine the pledge, I found the following core values:

- Faith—Service to God
- Accountability
- Hard work
- Generosity
- National and Global Service
- Loyalty
- Peace

- Justice
- Creativity
- Honesty/ Integrity
- Brotherhood
- Patriotism
- Advancement of Human Race

You can choose from this list or create your own by doing research on Google or simply write what's on your heart. Here is a list from Google:

- Peace of mind
- Transparency
- Innovation
- Efficiency
- Respect
- Education
- Optimism

- Diversity
- Human Dignity
- Consistency
- Courage
- Leadership
- Perseverance
- Compassion

DESIGN TO WIN ACTIVITIES

Steps to Create Your Action/Progress Plan:

In the previous chapter, we completed some of the elements of your ideal career and life plan. Now, we will complete the other elements and combine the previous ones to create a strategic action plan. The remaining steps are as follows:

1. Create a list of 5-6 core values to govern your life and career.

2. Write a statement or list of 3-6 words that would describe your **personal brand**—what you want to be known for and how you would want people to describe you when they hear your name. Do further research on branding, if you are not clear. There are many videos on YouTube which can help you in this quest.

3. Review your major life goals and ensure each goal is measureable.

4. Determine the obstacles and difficulties you will have to overcome to achieve these 5 major goals.

5. Determine the knowledge and skills that you will need to accomplish these 5 major goals.

6. Determine the people, groups, sources of finance and organizations whose cooperation you will require to achieve these 5 major goals.

7. Make a list of all of your answers and organize them by sequence and priority.

8. Use the sample **Career and Life Plan** provided to create your Detailed winning strategic plan for your top five goals over the next 1-5 years.

9. Include at least 3 pictures in your plan to represent your future.

10. Read the 10 tips to actualize your plans. Determine your chief goal from all your top 5 and list 3 actions you will take immediately over the next 10 days to begin to accomplish this goal.

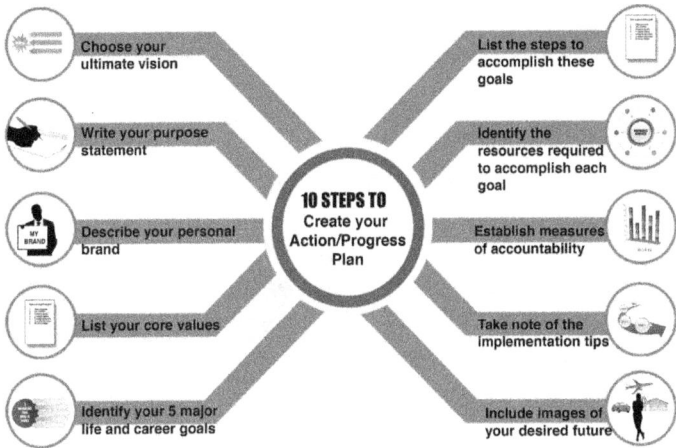

Choose your ultimate vision

Write your purpose statement

Describe your personal brand

List your core values

Identify your 5 major life and career goals

10 STEPS TO Create your Action/Progress Plan

List the steps to accomplish these goals

Identify the resources required to accomplish each goal

Establish measures of accountability

Take note of the implementation tips

Include images of your desired future

SAMPLE LIFE AND CAREER PLAN

JOHN SMITH
Entrepreneur

My Life and Career Plan
2018 – 2023

TABLE OF CONTENTS

PERSONAL BRAND
I am a very humble person who helps people to make their dreams come true.

LIFE VISION (DESTINATION)

- John Smith was a helpful man.
- By age 25, John finished his schooling and then went overseas to start his dream.
- After building his dream overseas through much hard work, he returned to Jamaica to open another company that sprays and fixes cars with the name of Smith's Auto Shop.
- John Smith retired by the age of 45.
- He is remembered for inspiring the younger generation.
- He fell in love with a lovely empress and got married. The union produced a beautiful daughter and a son.
- Smith was always jovial, realistic, determined, honest and caring.
- He gave back to his community.
- His legacy will live on through his works from now until eternity.

MY PURPOSE STATEMENT

I exist to add value to people's lives and create a revolution in the automotive industry.

MY CORE VALUES

1. Creativity
2. Innovation
3. Commitment
4. Honesty
5. Loyalty
6. Hard work
7. Humility

MY SHORT TERM GOALS (1-2 YEARS)
1. I buy a new car, Ford Focus, by 2020.
2. I have my Business Degree by 2018.
3. I have a good job paying of at least $80,000 by 2019.
4. I start to travel to Canada in 2019.
5. I start my automotive business in 2020 with some of my friends.

MY LONG TERM GOALS (3-5 YEARS)
1. I buy my parents a six bedroom home by 2023.
2. I migrate to Canada by 2021.
3. I have my own family by 2021.
4. I own a successful automotive business by 2023.
5. I travel the world in visiting at least 10 countries by 2023.

REASONS/REWARDS TO ACCOMPLISH GOALS
1. I have to make my parents proud.
2. I don't like to work for people, so that will push me harder to become an entrepreneur.
3. So that I can help others.
4. So that I can make my dreams come true.
5. So I can make the world a better place.

Action Plan Table

Goals	Steps to Accomplish	Resources	Accountability	Timeline	Results - Tick when accomplished
I have a business degree	Study, complete my work study, pass exams	Transportation cost, mainly - J$5,000 each week	My parents and best friend	2018	
I have a job at Toyota Jamaica	Go there on work study. Perform well and apply for a post shortly before graduation	Recommendation from supervisor, family and school contacts, resume. Degree	Parents	January 2019	
I migrate to Canada	Get visa, apply for job in Canada, work with travel agent, save the funds needed	Parents, travel agent, J$250,000	My parents	2021	
I have my automotive factory by 2023	Get a job so I can save Find a place Get tools, equipment Workers and resources	Loan from bank, help from parents and wife about J$10 - 15 million	My wife and parents can help me with finances	2023	
I travel to 10 countries	Go on a cruise and travel to individual countries. Make a list of the countries to travel, save money, visas, airfare	Travel agent, spouse's help, US$7,000	My wife	2023	

Pictures of My Future

HOW TO BRING
YOUR PLAN TO LIFE

"To plan without acting is futile"
—Myles Munroe

Life, like travelling, comes with its share of eventualities. There is a saying in Jamaica: "man plan and God wipe." This means that often times our plans do not work out, because they don't align with God's plan, and ultimately it is His purposes that will prevail. Many persons use this as an excuse not to plan. If we fail to plan, we are planning to fail. We should not wait until persons get sick before we train doctors and nurses and build hospitals. Success is never accidental; it's always intentional. Players on a sports team should not only know the team's plan but also execute it on the field of play.

As explained in our Travel Smart tips, we must be flexible with our plans and our timelines. We have to be patient, as often there are flight delays, detours and stormy weather which prevent travel. Patience will be needed. Remember: strong trees do not grow overnight, and anything of value takes time to build.

10 IMPLEMENTATION TIPS

1. *Act to Win.* You must take action on your plan. The farmer who does not plant cannot expect a harvest. As Nike says, "just do it!"

2. *Keep Your Goals in Sight.* Jim Rohn reminds us that "everything by longevity goes off track." Life is filled with many distractions, and things will

happen that will cause us to forget what is important to us. In this regard, you can do any of the following to keep the goals alive:

a) Create a vision board of the pictures and put it in a place that you can see it every day.
b) Use your phone to record a congratulatory note to yourself about reaching these goals in five years. Play this note daily.
c) Create a cue card of your goals and rewards and keep in your pocket/purse/wallet and look at it once or twice each day.
d) Daily rewrite these goals from memory and pray over them.

3. *Discipline Your Disappointments.* Along the way, there will be disappointments. Perhaps your goals or plan will take longer to materialize than you initially thought. If so, simply reset the timelines and learn the lessons along the way. Don't give up. Learn how to handle rejection and how to overcome obstacles.

4. *Get an Accountability Partner.* This will help to keep you on track.

5. *Success Models.* Learn from the masters. Listen to their stories, read their books. This will keep you inspired on the journey. Get a mentor or coach.

6. *Network and Collaborate with Others.* You may not have the resources but learn to become resourceful. Find out how to access resources. No one succeeds alone. No architect builds alone. Form a mastermind group if necessary. Join an

online group. Join associations of those in your field.

7. *Practise Self-Discipline.* This is the master key to success. It is the power to make yourself do what you ought to do, whether you feel like it or not. Take consistent action. It takes 10,000 hours of practice to develop mastery.

8. *Invest Continually in Your Personal Growth.* You may need to learn some new skills to implement your design. Read continually. Listen to audio books, attend seminars and continually work on your self-development, so you can lead the field and be compensated richly. As Jim Rohn said, "success is what you attract by the person you become." When you invest in your personal growth, you are making yourself attractive and fit for use.

9. *Develop Success Habits.* We are what we repeatedly do. John Maxwell talks about the law of 5. Everyday do 5 things that will lead to your success. Success habits include reading, managing your time properly, exercising, expressing gratitude and so much more. What's key is to develop a routine that will lead to your success. Find out the habits of successful people and make them part of your life.

10. *Be Patient, Persevere and Maintain a Positive Attitude.* If you quit, you will never win. There will be disappointments along the journey but keep going. It's not over until you win!

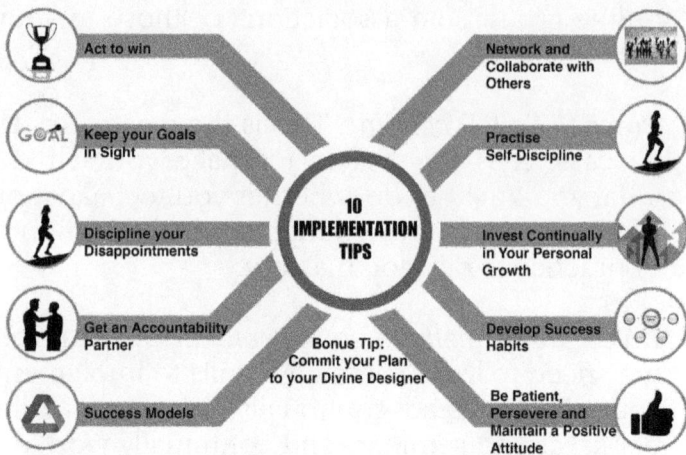

10 IMPLEMENTATION TIPS

- Act to win
- Keep your Goals in Sight
- Discipline your Disappointments
- Get an Accountability Partner
- Success Models
- Network and Collaborate with Others
- Practise Self-Discipline
- Invest Continually in Your Personal Growth
- Develop Success Habits
- Be Patient, Persevere and Maintain a Positive Attitude

Bonus Tip: Commit your Plan to your Divine Designer

PART III:
FUNDAMENTAL LIFE-
MANAGEMENT SKILLS

CHAPTER 13:
THE ART OF LIFE
HURDLING

"Adversity is the mother of progress"
—Mahatma Ghandi

All chapters in Part III, including this one, are based on Step 4 of the *Design to Win* process: **Development**. If we are to win in our lives and careers, there are some fundamental life-management skills which must be developed. These are the subjects of Chapters 13–16. They include: learning to deal with obstacles, failures and rejection; managing your time and becoming productive; developing success habits and managing your personal money.

Daryl Cross, author of *Dark Clouds at Work*, highlights Stanford research on the impact of technical skills versus interpersonal and communication skills on career success and business success. The findings show that interpersonal and communication skills, also known as *Emotional Intelligence*, carry much greater weight than technical skills. The percentage ratio is as follows: Technical skills (12.5%) and Interpersonal Skills (87.5%). This shows that while technical skills are important, your emotional intelligence is of even greater importance for life, career and business success. This is why in this book in Step 4 –Development, greater attention is focussed on life-management skills rather than technical skills to create a winning life and career.

BECOMING LIFE-HURDLING CHAMPIONS

In 1996, Deon Hemmings broke the Olympic record for the 400 metres hurdles and created history by becoming the first Jamaican female Olympic champion for this event. She won gold in a very difficult race which is quite a phenomenal achievement. Jamaica's famous world leading athlete, Usain Bolt repeatedly refused to specialize in the 400 metres, because the training for that event was even more gruelling than training for the 100 or 200 metres races. Hurdling, is not so much about running but about a technique to cross over obstacles to get to the finish line. Athletes can be disqualified in these races if the technique is not properly followed.

In the same way, our success in life is very much dependent on learning the techniques or strategies to overcome the hurdles or obstacles that life will throw at us. This reminds me of a quote by author Charles R. Swindoll: "LIFE IS 10% what happens to you and 90% how you react to it." It is as author Jim Rohn says: "it's not the wind that blows, but the set of the sail."

Successful life hurdling is about learning to set a better sail. It is about learning to overcome the obstacles that threaten to impede your progress. It is about being determined to win gold in life, no matter what happens. It is about learning to handle disappointments, misfortune, setbacks, failures, losses and other forms of adversity like a champion. It is about turning tragedies into triumph and profiting from failure.

The art of life hurdling is one of the necessary skills to be learnt as part of Step 4 (Development) in creating a winning life and career. It is as the book of James says, learning to "count it all joy when you fall into various trials" knowing that your trials are building patience and endurance. Endurance, as theologian William Barclay notes, "is not just the ability to bear a hard thing, but to turn it into glory."

The Barclay quote was the catalyst for my writing in April 2014, after my devastating relational breakup. I was engaged to be married for the second time in my life, and it all fell apart after my wedding dress was bought, hotel booked, church booked and photography package down payment made. I had to learn how to overcome that hurdle. The good news is that I did successfully overcome it using certain life-hurdling keys. And the good news is that like Deon Hemmings, you, too, can learn the keys to successfully leap over your life hurdles and become a life-hurdling champion.

RUTH'S LIFE-HURDLING MAP

The letters in the word "MAP" help us to remember seven keys to overcome a hurdle. I began sharing these keys in youth presentations at churches in Jamaica, and in 2017, I shared them in a workshop in Uganda with 22 church leaders. In every case, the presentation was well received. Three testimonials will be shared later in this chapter. The hurdles we face may fall under one of the following seven categories:

1. Spiritual Hurdles
2. Mental and Emotional Hurdles
3. Financial and Material Hurdles
4. Physical Hurdles
5. Relational Hurdles
6. Education and Career Hurdles
7. Personal or Social/Community Hurdles

The 10 keys offered here can help us to successfully overcome any of these hurdles and enable us to win gold in the race of life.

Mindset Shift: I have found that one of the secrets of transformation and overcoming any hurdle is our mind and how we think. Dr. Caroline Leaf, a renowned cognitive neuroscientist and author, has conducted research on the mind for over 25 years. She explains that we can rewire our brains and that our thinking affects our health. On her website she writes, "75% to 95% of the illnesses that plague us today are a direct result of our thought life. What we think about affects us physically and emotionally. It's an epidemic of toxic emotions."

Her studies underscore the point that it is not so much what happens to us but how we think about it that determines whether we rise or fall. When negative things happen to us, we often develop toxic thinking, which can also be considered negative thinking. If our interpretation of our adversity is negative, it will be harder to overcome. No wonder that William Barclay's quote became a catalyst for my recovery.

I believe our adversities, are gifts of greatness in disguise. I know this is extremely hard to grasp when you are going through adversity. How can rape, murder and abuse serve any good purpose? I do not believe those things in and of themselves are good but you can repurpose your pain. As Napoleon Hill says, "find the seed of equivalent benefit in it." After you have cried and bled, you must take measures to heal, and one of those is repurposing your pain by changing your thinking.

A mindset shift means that we live with the expectancy of adversity. Obstacles are inevitable and, rather than wishing them away, we should prepare for them and create a response strategy in advance. It makes no sense when we argue with the sunshine or the seasons of life. Arguing about the seasons will not change anything. If you expect rain, walk with an umbrella. It means instead of asking "why me?" and thinking that the pain has come to kill you, that you see these as building blocks. It means we take on the attitude that Jim Rohn espoused: "Don't wish it was easier, wish you were better. Don't wish for less problems, wish for more skills. Don't wish for less challenge, wish for more wisdom." This shift in mindset has aided my recovery time and time again.

Attitude: It is our attitude that will determine whether we become a life-hurdling champion or not. In my presentations, I normally demonstrate this by having two persons tackle one person who is trying to reach an object of their desire in order to win a prize. In every case, the outcome is attitude-based. If the "obstacles/-blockers" feel that the pursuer is too strong for them, the pursuer wins. If the pursuer feels that despite the size of the blockers/obstacles, he can win, he usually does, or keeps persevering until the clock runs out. I normally give the pursuer a time to reach the prize. A positive attitude goes a far way in overcoming life's hurdles.

Association: Every athlete needs a coach, and everyone who is faced with a challenge needs support to overcome it. We are like banana trees. Sometimes the load of bearing fruit gets heavy, and we begin to lean under the strain. Like the banana tree, we need a stick to hold us up, so we can bear fruit and fulfil our purpose. We cannot bear the loads of life alone. Don't be afraid to ask for help. Reach out before you crumble. Kelly McGonnigle in her TED talk, How to Make Stress Your Friend, explains that "stress makes you social." When we undergo stress, oxytocin (the 'cuddle' hormone) is released. During stress, your body is calling for association. Furthermore, she notes, "Oxytocin is also received in the heart, to strengthen, heal and protect it from the effects of stress."

Affirmation: Closely akin to association is affirmation. The affirming words of others can help us to overcome our adversity. The trouble is like the friends of the biblical character Job, many people unwittingly say harmful and hurtful things during our bereavement, failure or loss. In cases like these, it would be better to keep ones mouth shut. As motivational speaker Les Brown notes, "toxic people can ruin your life." It was the affirming words of my mentor, Rev. Courtney Richards, and others who helped me to overcome that relational loss in 2014. To this day, I remember Rev. Richards's words: "You are loved, prized and valued." Affirm someone today with your words and actions. Your words may enable them to become a life-hurdling champion.

Action: You have to participate in your recovery. Are you repeatedly facing particular hurdles because there is something in you that needs to change? If for example, you keep having relational failures, it's time to look into the mirror and create an action plan for change. If you keep getting fired, don't feel sorry for yourself; change the course of your actions. You have to act to win. Acting might include seeking counselling and psychotherapy. Acting might mean setting up boundaries, exercising, changing your diet, etc. In the midst of your pain, consider carefully what actions you must take for healing.

Purpose: We have already spoken extensively on this one. As a reminder, purpose helps you to overcome pain. It is what enables you to persevere. Dr. Victor Frankl, a Nazi Holocaust survivor, noted that those who survived the experience were those who had a deep sense of purpose.

Profitability: This particular key in the workshops is usually the most memorable. I often challenge the participants to find the silver lining in several devastating situations. How could those situations bring profit or be a gift in disguise? I usually give them real life examples such as: Nelson Mandela, whose 27 years in prison and struggle against Apartheid eventually led him to the presidency of South Africa and gave him world-renown; Joyce Meyer was sexually abused by her father for years and now uses her story to empower others; Jesus the Christ's murder in Christian theology eventually bought salvation and the gift of eternal life. I also use my experiences and scars which have now become my stars and taken me to places I never dreamt of going as a child. Sometimes our hurdles also bring us financial profit. Singer-song writer Adele, penned her relational pain and produced an album that brought her millions in financial gain. I have written and sold books which have become a platform for income and impact.

Progress Planning: This is akin to taking action. Recovery, like success, is not accidental. There is a need to plan for our progress in the face of adversity. Where do you go from here? What is the way forward? If you fail to plan, there will be no progress. For example, having lost your job, now what? Now that you are divorced, what's next? You have lost your loved one, what's next? You have been diagnosed with an illness, now what? Leaping over these hurdles requires planning for your progress. Whether we have hurdles or not in life, when we feel like we are not progressing, we become unhappy. Progress is one of the needs of our core being.

Past Successes: There is an unbelievable boost that comes from thinking about past successes when facing a current hurdle.

The point is that our victories in the past are fodder for tomorrow's victories. If we did it back then, we have what it takes to do it now. Sometimes these are not necessarily our personal victories; they can be the stories of others who faced similar challenges and triumphed. Their testimonies inspire us, spark our creativity and give us hope that we too can rise above our adversity. I remember in 2017, when I was scheduled to travel to Uganda and South Africa, the expense of the mission was daunting. At times, I felt it was not possible. Then I remembered that in 2013, the expenses were greater, and yet it was done. That past victory motivated me, and in the end, I made the trip.

Prayer: This, friends, is my greatest life-hurdling tool. There are some challenges which hit us that are no match for mere mortals, and only a Higher Power, a Supreme being can help us to overcome. The magnitude of some hurdles require divine intervention. However, whether the obstacle be great or small, prayer helps us to recover faster and become resilient. There are studies that have shown the positive effects of prayer on the sick and those facing adversities. If there is one thing I know in the face of obstacles, is that after I have prayed, even if the problem is not solved, my mindset and heart shift; peace comes over me after crying out to God in prayer for help. I encourage you to use this powerful life-hurdling key as one of the key techniques to become a life-hurdling champion.

For more life-hurdling keys, get my book *Keys to Win at Life: 100 Proven Ways to Handle Life's Challenges.*

RUTH'S RECAP
LIFE-HURDLING TECHNIQUE

In addition to the 10 keys which have been shared, there is a simple life-hurdling technique which I have used in as little as 5 minutes to overcome disappointments and day-to-day obstacles. I also use it as a counselling and personal coaching tool when others come to me with their life challenges. The ReCAP acronym describes a 7-step process to create a mind-shift which eventually causes a change in our emotions and behaviour. It produces insights that relieve anxiety and bring emotional healing.

Think of a recent challenge—a disappointment, setback, heartbreak, an incident, sad news, bad report that robbed you of your joy. This could be at home, work, school, church or relational.

Recount the incident briefly. What happened?

Capture your thoughts and feelings about the incident. Write statements or list these on a sheet of paper. If talking to someone, you can vocalize your thoughts and feelings.

Analyze each of those thoughts and feelings for truth and replace them or the dominant negative thought or feeling (often this is a lie) with a truth statement or a positive statement.

Affirm yourself out loud with truth statements or positive statements.

Process for Profit; list 1-3 ways to profit from this hurdle by considering one or all of the questions below:

- Is there anything to be grateful for in this situation?
- Is there any benefit in this situation?
- Can anything good come out of this situation?
- How could this lead to profit whether financial, societal or for your own development?
- Is there any lesson that can be learnt from this situation?
- Is there any opportunity that this experience affords for good?

Progress Planning; consider the possibilities for profit, and create a strategy to profit from this situation. What will you do to make progress? How will you move forward? Write at least one action you will take or steps for progress.

Pray about the situation—your thoughts, feelings and plans.

THE ART OF LIFE-HURDLING
WORKSHOP TESTIMONIALS

Feedback from some of the young people at Calvary Gospel Assembly in Kingston, Jamaica:

It was informative and shows a lot of real life aspects....Aunty Cameka Keep doing the good work and keep on holding on (sic).

Loved the activities and this event was beneficial to my personal growth (sic).

I would have wanted it to be a little longer. It was very interesting. A lot of aspects can be used as a life change within my life (sic).

CHAPTER 14:
HOW TO DEAL WITH
FAILURE AND REJECTION

Allow the breeze that brought a maize
plant down to strengthen it.
—African Proverb

A GAME OF DOMINOES

One of our favourite pastimes in Jamaica is playing a game of dominoes. This is a board game that men especially love to play, and on weekends, we can find Jamaican men all around the island playing a game of dominoes. What's more, I recently discovered that children also have a love for dominoes, especially the young boys. I believe this is something we can capitalize on in a number of ways. My friend Rev. Carla Dunbar has capitalized on men's love for dominoes and has used it in her work of evangelism to lead men to faith in Jesus Christ. I, too, have now found a way to use dominoes to teach life skills or keys to win at life, dominoes have been speaking to me on how to handle rejection and failure. Here is the story of how this happened.

One afternoon, while volunteering with the Child Resiliency programme (a violence prevention alliance initiative), I saw one of my boys with a pack of dominoes. He wanted to play dominoes during class, but I could not facilitate him that evening. However, I promised to do so at another time. I knew I had to find a legitimate way to include it into my teaching plan, but I was not sure how to do so. Well, on one particular evening, the life skills topic was: "How to Deal with Rejection," and I knew instantly that the time had come to play dominoes! The idea came to me to use dominoes to teach them about handling rejection, and I know by now you are quite intrigued to find out how. Well, you are not alone! One of our counsellors raised his eyebrows when I shared the idea, but after I explained it to him, he was totally blown away!

As usual, I researched my topic and looked for three key lessons or ways to develop each skill. Now, because I want to keep the story short, I encourage you to research the game of dominoes and its rules if you are unfamiliar with dominoes. Suffice to say, in its simplest form, the game is about matching pieces of tiles with numbers. A domino is any of 28 small oblong pieces marked with 0–6 pips in each half. The game usually has four players, who each select (draw) seven random domino tiles. Each player then takes turn to match the pieces. The player who finishes his hand first, wins. If however, the game is blocked, meaning there are no more matches, the player with the lowest count wins. You would add all the pips of your remaining dominoes to get your count.

Moreover, there are times in the game when a player has no matching pieces when it's his turn to play; the player will exclaim: "Pass!" It's in a sense a game of chance. Players can pass several times, but eventually their time to play will come again. It's important to remember that when a player selects his seven pieces of dominoes that he does not see the numbers on the tiles. Thus, he cannot control the tile selection. What's more, a player can lose a match but that does not mean that he will lose the game. If he continues playing, he will learn from his mistakes and may even eventually win the game. These facts are important if we are to learn how to handle rejection and failure from a game of dominoes.

THE PAIN OF
REJECTION AND FAILURE

Experiences of rejection and failure—regardless of the context or reason—are very painful. I recently learnt that rejection activates the same pain center in the body as being physically wounded. This pain is both emotional and physical, and I have experienced both. Relational rejections hurt like a deep knife wound in the heart, especially when the relational ties are strong. When a relationship fails, it is equally damaging. Divorce for example is an extremely painful experience that can have prolonged negative effects for years to come.

How can dominoes teach resilience? Here are five lessons from the game in learning to handle rejection and failure.

1. Don't Take Rejection/Failure Personally—You have no control over your "hand."

A huge part of handling rejection is learning to control your thinking and developing a proper perspective. In the game of dominoes, the player has no control over the hand he has been dealt. Thus if he has no matching piece and cannot play, he should not take it personally. Often times when rejected, it may not be your fault. If for example, you are rejected because of your race, looks, social standing or some physical feature, then it's not your fault. You have no control over the "hand" you have been given by life. Sometimes you are rejected because someone does not know you or because the situation is not working for them, so they have to "pass" on it.

This is where hope and proper perspective are necessary, because even if you pass, you can still win. We can bear this in mind when dealing with failure and rejection. Failing at something does not make you a failure and it's important to know the difference. The failure may indeed be in your best interest. It may be telling you to pass on this one. It may not be the right opportunity. It may not be the right time or person. That failure, rejection or "pass" may in turn lead to the right opportunity at a later point. When one door closes, another one opens, so do not take it personally.

2. Reframe Your Thinking—Eventually, Your Match Will Come

In the game of dominoes, when you "pass" it simply means that the domino does not fit, because there are no matching pieces. When a relationship ends, try to see it as just that. It simply was not a match or it was a bad fit. For one reason or another, it required a "pass." When you fail to get the promotion or are repeatedly rejected in your job-hunting, bear in mind the game of dominoes. See it as a "pass." Remember, a pass does not mean that a player can never play again. Even if it occurs repeatedly, eventually the player's match comes and he can play. Say to yourself: "Eventually my match will come. Eventually, I will get it right. Eventually I will find the right fit." This particular relationship/-situation may not have worked, but who says the game is over? Your match may still be out there, and you may still get it right.

3. Don't Give Up—You Can Still Win

As my children learnt, it is important to keep a level head when you "pass," because you can still win the game. One of my students experienced this in the game. He became upset at first when he had to "pass," but in the end he won the game. Furthermore, in the simplest form of the game, there are six rounds, and just because a player may lose one or two rounds, it does not mean he cannot win the game. He just needs to be patient and regroup. My students experienced this as well. Here are two real life examples using famous Hollywood stars: Mickey Rooney married eight times and divorced six times; Jennifer O'Neil has had nine marriages, and she has stayed with husband number nine since 1996. There is still hope for me and you! Don't despair in the face of failure. You can learn and change, and you can still win!

4. See Rejection / Failure as a Chance to Improve

In the game of dominoes, one must learn to read the game. When you can read the game well, you have a better chance of winning. When you are rejected or have failed, you should see it as a chance to learn to improve yourself. My relational rejections and failures have taught me so much about myself. Because of them, I now have a better sense of self-worth. I am actually making wiser decisions as a result. I am now studying and spending time with those who are doing well relationally, so that I can do better next time. I am learning to read the game of relationships and studying to improve my game.

5. Acknowledge the Pain; Accept it and Move On

In the game of dominoes, as with all games, there are winners and losers. Losing is painful and not many people handle it well. Whatever you do, in the face of rejection and failure, don't deny the pain but do not let it get the best of you. Determine to become better not bitter, powerful not pitiful. Take the time you need to heal and find a positive way of handling the rejection and failure. The sooner you accept your loss or failure and move on, the better it will be. In the game of dominoes, you can choose to continue playing or give someone else a chance.

In our life-skill class, we have approximately 10-12 students and I usually ask the losing party to allow others to play. Those who are not good at playing do not mind. They would rather do something else. Their attitude taught me another lesson. We can take the same approach to relationship failures and rejection or any other matter that does not give the right result. When it does not work, move on to something else or someone else. That something may be a new career or a new focus.

5 Ways to Deal With Failure and Rejection

It's Only a Pass. Don't take rejection/failure personally. Sometimes you have no control over your "hand."

Reframe Your Thinking - Eventually, your match will come.

Don't Give Up - You can still win.

See Rejection/Failure as a chance to improve.

Acknowledge the pain. Accept it and move on.

THE SUCCESS HABITS CHALLENGE

One of the techniques that I have used to recover from failure is the use of challenges to change my habits. The development of success habits is an important aspect of Step 4 of our Design to Win process. "We become what we repeatedly do," according to Sean Covey, author of the 7 Habits of Highly Effective Teens. Covey accurately sums up what this key is about. A habit is what we repeatedly do, and what we repeatedly do daily eventually tells the tale of our lives. According to Charles Duhigg in *The Power of Habits*, habits are formed as a result of cues, routines and rewards. Habits shape our character and destiny.

Both successful and unsuccessful people have habits. The idea is to find out what are the habits of successful people and adopt them as well as avoid the habits of unsuccessful people in order to win at life. As part of my *Design to Win* initiatives, I usually have a 21-day Success Habits Challenge in January of each year, where I encourage persons to practice 5 habits over 21 days that are vital to their success.

The following is a list of 10 common success habits from which we choose:

1. Rising Early
2. Daily Reading
3. Expressing Gratitude
4. Daily Rewriting Goals
5. Regular Exercise
6. A Morning Routine
7. Meditation
8. Solitude
9. Keeping a Journal

10. Practising Self-control

The idea to use five (5) habits came from noted leadership expert John Maxwell's Rule of Five (5). In one of his presentations, Maxwell asked, "What if I use an axe to chop a tree just five times a day, will the tree eventually fall?" Of course it will eventually fall! In the same way, the Rule of 5 is simply a series of activities that you do every day that are fundamental to your success. For John, his five rules are as follows: *every day he reads, every day he files, every day he thinks, every day he asks questions and every day he writes.* May you find your rule of five (5) habits that will help you win at life!

However, one does not have to restrict it to those success habits. Recently, participants in the FIT programme—a career and life empowerment initiative—engaged in a *Millionaire Habits Challenge*. In this challenge, they were encouraged to practise one of the money management strategies learnt for 21 days. They apportioned an allotted sum of money daily using an agreed upon money management strategy. These challenges built the participants' muscles of perseverance and consistency, which are now vital to their success.

Personally, I use challenges to change my habits and sometimes it goes beyond 21 days to years. I have engaged in food restriction challenges, relationship fasts, transportation challenges and exercise challenges, etc. These challenges have changed my life. I would encourage you to do a personal challenge as well. I guarantee that it will be quite rewarding. It will even boost your self-esteem and confidence.

Chapter 15:
Time-Management and
Productivity Hacks

In 2016, I followed Dr. Eric Thomas's You-Tube channel for a season. I was very inspired by the hip hop preacher's story. The name of the program is TGIM, which means, "Thank God It's Monday!" No, not TGIF or "Thank God it's Friday." ET looks forward to Monday as it is represents the start of the period to go after his dreams each week. Similarly, Monday is a day I look forward to after a long weekend but for a different reason. I know most of us do not look forward to Mondays, because it's back to work. However, Monday is my day of rest. It is the time I withdraw from work and renew my reserves to be more productive from Tuesday through Sunday. This has been part of the routine and strategy that has increased my output and decreased my stress level. In this chapter, I will share the importance of rest and sleep as well as six other amazing, stress reducing, productivity and time management strategies to boost your success. The sensational seven hacks are as follows:

1. Advanced Planning with Must Dos
2. Eliminate Online Distraction

3. Create 1 hour of Undisturbed Time for Work Daily
4. Track Your Time and Apprehend the Time Wasting Culprits
5. Outsource and Delegate
6. Learn to Say "No"
7. Make Times of Rest a Priority

How do you build a business and work part-time? How do you work and study at the same time? In our busy world, how do you manage a full-time job, family and social responsibilities without stressing out yourself, and yet remain productive, healthy and happy? The seven hacks are proven ways that have helped me and many others to hurdle these challenges quite well. When you become an excellent time manager, you will feel good about yourself, because you feel you have "control" over your time. A major cause of stress is a sense of not having control over your time, and when you take on new responsibilities, you have to adjust your routine. Some of us don't adjust well to new responsibilities. These hacks will be help to remedy this situation.

Advance Planning with Must Dos

According to time management expert Brian Tracy, "every minute spent in planning saves 10 minutes in execution." He encourages persons to always plan before they act. Success expert Jim Rohn says, "You must see your day before it begins. See your week before it begins." I refer to this as, "Designing the day to seize the day." My advance planning technique includes making a list of all my tasks to be done for the week (sometimes the next 100 days) and a list of my Must Do Tasks for each day or week. To manage your time well, you must recognize that there is not enough time to do everything you want to do, but there is sufficient time to do what is most important to you. In following Tracy's expert advice, ask yourself the following questions:

- What have I been hired to do?
- What is the most valuable use of my time?
- What results matter?
- What am I trying to accomplish each day and why?
- Which 20% of my activities will give me 80% results?

After figuring these out, create a schedule of 5-6 key activities to be done each day and check mark your must dos for each day. Tracy in his book, *Eat That Frog*, encourages us to do our most important task first. This task very often is not pleasant and is akin to eating a frog.

In my case, I don't always do my most important/difficult task first. However, I am careful to make sure as much as possible that my must dos are done daily or weekly, and I usually get them done. Time management requires discipline and determination. Tracy notes that it's best to start off with the most important task for that day before attempting any other, because if you cannot finish everything on that list, at least getting that one out the way will make you feel accomplished.

Additionally, planning in advance eases my stress and helps me to sleep better. I don't have to wonder what to do the next day. What's more, I find this type of planning on a Friday helps me to relax on the weekends or focus on my speaking assignments and time with family and friends. It can also be done at the end of each work day, just before going to bed or within the first hour of the day, before you start daily activities. Now, do try this hack and let me know if it works for you.

ELIMINATE ONLINE DISTRACTION

Social media is a major time waster these days. If you can avoid checking your email or going on Facebook before leaving for work or school and before accomplishing your top must do activity, you will be more productive. All of us know when we begin checking emails and Facebook that 15 minutes quickly turns into 2 hours. If I want to reach work on time, it is best not to go on social media early in the morning.

Here are some suggestions to eliminate or decrease the distractions: turn off your notifications, set specific times to check emails and messages, perhaps 2-3 times a day and turn off your WIFI for set periods. Exception to these guidelines may be if your work directly involves social media or you work online. I know this is extremely hard, but if we are to focus and be productive, we cannot allow the gadgets to rule us. We must master the gadgets.

Research done by Harvard scientists in 2012 revealed the negative effects of the constant use of online gadgets on our brains and lives. These devices—including our Smartphones and tablets—are turning us into addicts just as if we were on crack cocaine. These devices produce dopamine, a feel-good but addictive hormone. The problem for Millennials is that they are addicted to their devices, and this reduces innovation and the ability to focus and think creatively. It is pretty interesting to note, according to author Simon Sinek in his famous interview about *Millennials in the Workplace*, that...

> *Many of the elite in tech such as Steve Jobs and Evan Williams never allowed their children to use iPads or cellphones knowing full well what the outcome would be from constant usage. They were well aware of the correlation of addiction with technology and the dopamine cellphones release in our brains.*

It is time we take this seriously and do our best to eliminate unnecessary online distractions. Doing this will improve our productivity and our time management.

CREATE 1 HOUR OF UNDISTURBED TIME FOR WORK DAILY

The reality is many persons do not do productive work during the scheduled working hours on the job each day. Many employees waste time doing things unrelated to their jobs such as checking social media pages, engaging in idle talk or gossip and taking extended lunch breaks. Those who operate in an office environment also know that unplanned meetings or unscheduled walk-ins often hinder our daily productivity. As success expert Brian Tracy recommends, create one (1) hour of undisturbed time to work on your major tasks. This, he explains will amount to three (3) full days of regular work. So how do we achieve this? Here are some suggestions:

1. Arrive at work earlier or work later except when working by hourly wage requiring "clock-in/-out" or submitted time sheet that affects payroll.
2. If you have an office, where permitted put up a "no disturb" or "meeting in progress" sign.
3. Turn off your WIFI or put your phone on silent.
4. Ask your secretary or relevant person to hold all calls for an hour except for emergencies.
5. Let persons know your undisturbed times, so they do not interrupt except for a work related emergency.
6. Start your day earlier before everyone else rises and get the work done before you leave home.

Finally, notes Tracy, when you are at work, "work all the time you work." When you don't work all the time you are at work, you have to take work home. This encroaches on your family time and robs them of your valuable presence.

Track Your Time and Apprehend the Time Wasting Culprits

According to Brian Tracy, "time management is life management." In order to be an effective time manager, you must desire it, decide to act, be disciplined and determined, or it will not work. One of the ways to increase and improve your time management is by *tracking your time and apprehending time wasting culprits.*

If time is money, then we need to know how we spend it. What if you had a business and never knew where the money went month after month and week after week? I'm sure that would be a recipe for disaster, so why are we so casual about our time? No wonder we are stressed! If you don't know concretely how you are spending your time, there is no way you can concretely determine how to save, trim or redirect energies and activities.

Moreover, tracking is a good way to assess any area of your life that is causing stress. Just the notion of observation makes you more careful in your actions. In 2015, I tracked my time for the week and noted my activities for each hour and then at the end of the week; I did an assessment. I knew I spent a lot of time on the internet, but I was shocked by the number of hours, and it was not all on productive activities. I realized that even though I need to work online, I could make that time more efficient by scheduling set times for research or socializing.

Tracking works! I did the same thing with my finances and tracked my expenditures over the course of 31 days. Once again, I was shocked at how much I was spending on transportation. Since then, I have been able to reduce my travel costs by 60%.

If you want to get control of your time, you've got to know concretely where it all goes. Only then can you apprehend the time wasting culprits and begin to take corrective measures. I would recommend tracking every quarter to measure your progress. Try it and let me know your results.

OUTSOURCE AND DELEGATE

Have you read *The 4-Hour Work Week* by Timothy Ferris? This is a fantastic book, if you desire to be more productive. Two of the concepts it discusses are "outsourcing" and "delegating." According to productivity specialist Michael Hyatt, you should delegate something, if you find someone who can do it 70% as well as you. Many persons struggle with delegation because of perfectionist tendencies, trust issues and concerns about quality. If you expand your services and intend to be very successful, you will need to delegate. You cannot succeed alone. Yes, it will take time to teach before you delegate, but in the end, it will save you time.

Outsourcing is similar. It is directing/sending the task to someone else who is more competent and skilled than you are or simply because you prefer not to be saddled with it. You can outsource subtasks to free up time to work on your main task. For example, Amazon is a great outsourcing platform which sells and distributes my books all over the world. This saves me from the stress of delivery and shipping. Fiverr (http://www.fiverr.com) is another great outsourcing site, where you can find qualified persons to do various tasks at an affordable rate. I use them to outsource much of my book publishing process, and it makes my life easier.

When outsourcing and delegating, you must act with clarity. Be very, very clear on what you want and describe this in great detail, so that the person or company can follow your instructions well. Having a virtual assistant is another means of outsourcing or delegating. We can hire virtual assistants to get some administrative tasks done at a fairly cheap rate. These virtual assistants can be in different time zones. In this way, while we sleep, someone is working on a task important to us, which will be ready when we start our work day in our own time zone. The things you do not like to do, that are not in line with your expertise should be outsourced or delegated. I generally outsource parts of my projects, and this both reduces my stress and increases my productivity. However, outsourcing and delegating can increase your stress level, if you do not give clear instructions and set strict deadlines. This, too, has been my experience.

LEARN TO SAY "NO"

Believe it or not, learning to say "no" is a major productivity, time management and stress reducing hack. You must learn to say no to activities that are of lower value that do not contribute greatly to your highest value tasks. Remember the Pareto Principle: only 20% of what you do contributes to 80% of your results. Make your yeses fewer and your nos more. Now if you are going to do this, be prepared for some backlash. Remember, if you want to reduce your stress and be more productive, less is more. You cannot attend every party or be there for everyone.

Use the Pareto Principle to identify the relationships, business activities, goals etc. which mean the most to you. Once you identify your yes activities, develop the courage to say no. From now on, ask yourself daily as Tracy teaches, "What is the most valuable use of my time right now?" This will keep you on track. Try it and see if it will increase your output and reduce your stress. Check out Gary Ryan Blair's video on YouTube on "The Power of No" to help you in learning to say no.

MAKING TIMES OF REST A PRIORITY

I was shocked to learn in productivity expert Michael Hyatt's book, *Unleashing Nature's Secret Weapon*, that going on six hours of sleep or less reduces your function to the level of someone who is legally drunk. There is a saying, "if you snooze, you lose," but according to Hyatt, those who "sleep at night, soar in the day." Skimping on sleep, says Hyatt, "impairs our mental performance, creates fatigue, inability to focus, slows reaction times and much more... Sleep refreshes our emotional state and boosts our immune system" (2017, 5-7). The effects of sleeplessness are significant.

We all know the adage, "All rest and no play makes Jack a dull boy," and it is true. Lack of rest reduces innovation and productivity. Sometime ago, a friend of mine called me and expressed how tired she was and how much she was in need of rest. She reported that she had become forgetful and was suffering from fatigue. She could not think clearly anymore from being overworked. She, however, admired the fact that I take one day off to rest. I told her that was non-negotiable for me. I will not ruin my life by not taking time off to rest. Monday is my preferred day off, because I work on the weekends.

Creatives like me need to take time off to renew our creative energies. This need is not only for Creatives. Our bodies are like phones and computers; we need to recharge often. An article in the Harvard Business Review by Tony Shwartz on *Productivity* makes the case quite well:

> *As every great athlete understands, the highest performance occurs when we balance work and effort with rest and renewal. The human body is hard-wired to pulse, and requires renewal at regular intervals not just physically, but also mentally and emotionally. Unfortunately, rest and renewal get no respect in the organizational world. Instead, most managers instinctively view those who seem to need time for rest and renewal as slackers. But what*

are the costs of working continuously? Do we think as clearly, creatively and strategically, or work as effectively with colleagues and clients, in the 10th or 12th or 14th hour of a workday devoid of real breaks, as you do in the 2nd or the 4th?

As a believer in making rest a priority to reduce stress and increase productivity, here is what I suggest. At the start of the year—or right now—set your days off or vacation times first and plan everything else around them. View these days and times as a reward and work towards them. Here is a formula shared by Brian Tracy in his book *Focal Point* in terms of the rest/work balance ratio.

a) Take 1 day off from work: spend time with family and on personal pursuit. Do not do work; read about work or work on computer. Let your brain recharge and rejuvenate from regular work.

b) Expand the time to 2 days and a full weekend over time.

c) Plan 3 days vacation every 3 months.

d) Plan 2-week vacations with family every year— reorder your life, so you have more time with family.

Now, here's to your productivity, better time management and reduced stress!

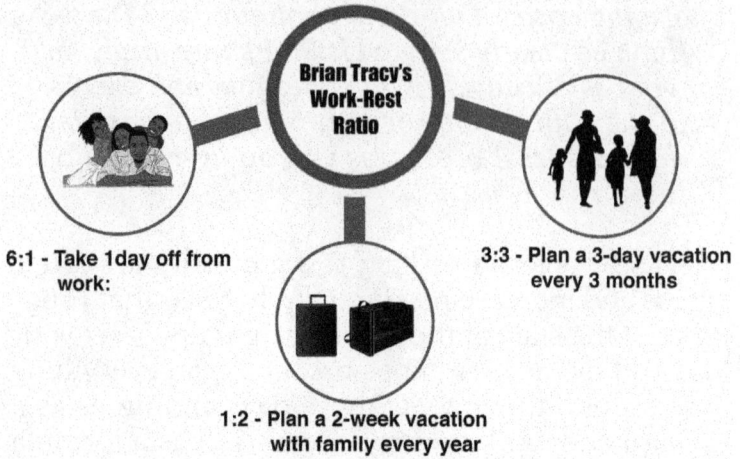

6:1 - Take 1day off from
work:

3:3 - Plan a 3-day vacation
every 3 months

1:2 - Plan a 2-week vacation
with family every year

CHAPTER 16:
MILLIONAIRE MONEY MAPS

*In the house of the wise are stores of
choice food and oil, but a foolish man
devours all he has .*
—Bible Proverb

BEING MONEY SMART

I f there is ever an area in life that people need to learn to be effective, this is surely one! The management of money is an essential life skill that all of us should get right early on. Unfortunately, most of us were never directly taught this valuable skill. Over and over the studies show that the majority of people are living from pay cheque to pay cheque. Jokes abound about our JOB (Just Over Broke) and the reality is: very often it's not that we don't make money, or have money pass through our fingers... it's just that it keeps passing through. Either we don't know how to spend it, or we don't have enough of it. Most of us don't generally understand the principles of money management.

The problem is compounded even more in that, even if we mentally understand it, very often our behaviour is just the opposite. It is for this reason that financial expert Dave Ramsey says, "Personal finances is 20% head knowledge and 80% behaviour." This is one area in which I have not for the most part exercised much wisdom, and I have paid a lot of stupid taxes (interest through indebtedness, bad habits and poor thinking about money). I am now finally on the winning path with money. Thanks to a decision to become money smart, and the consequences of just being sick and tired of struggling or losing in this area.

MONEY MANAGEMENT SERIES

In January 2018, I taught a two-week money management series entitled, "The Biblical Money MAP" at a friend's church. The series was so impactful that some participants shared with me a few days after that they had begun to apply one of the money management systems. Consequently, I decided to share a modified version of these workshops with members of my FIT programme. These are young men ages 18-35. We looked at the "Millionaire Mind" and "Millionaire Money Management Systems and Habits." They were very excited about it. The FIT teaching series lasted three (3) weeks followed by a 21-Day Millionaire Habits Challenge to utilize one of the money management systems. In the third workshop, one young man asked, "Why was this not taught in high school?" Then he said, "Miss, you should be paid to teach this in all the high schools."

While his comments were flattering, they also resonated with me. I decided to include some of the teachings from these series in this book. The Money MAP, like other MAPs shared in this book thus far, is an acronym. Each letter represents a key principle.

Mindset and Management: What does money mean to you? Who is the master of your money? Do you have a rich mindset or a poor mindset? Do you know how to manage money? If so, what system are you using? Money is not evil. It is the love of money that is evil. It is money that enables us to eat, educate ourselves, take care of our health, etc. However, money is like fire. It can be useful or dangerous, positive or negative. It's the heart and mind of the person handling the money which determines its best/worst use.

Money must be handled with care, or it will destroy you. It is a tool for good or evil. Money—like your life—belongs to God (1 Chronicles 29). God is the owner of it all; we are just managers/-trustees. God gives you money according to your management ability. We don't all get the same amount. If you manage what you have well, more will be given. If you don't, you will lose it. Jesus taught us not to worry about our daily needs but to seek first God's kingdom and all we need will be added (Matthew 6:33).

Attitude: How do you feel about money? Is it a good thing or an evil thing? How do you treat people when they have or do not have money? How does the absence of money affect you?

Beware of greed, the lure/deceitfulness of riches and the love of money. Your life is not measured in the abundance of things. Be careful of building wealth just for yourself and at the expense of your soul. Don't be selfish with your wealth. Be gener-ous. Don't be a rich fool. Don't be financially rich and relationally and spiritually bankrupt. It does not profit to gain the whole world and lose your soul (Mark 8:36).

Purpose, **Plan and Practice:** Do you know the purposes of money and how do you use it? Generally speaking money is to be used to take care of your personal needs and your family's needs; in service to humanity, building God's Kingdom [including paying God's workers]; and being our brother's keeper, that is, to support the poor and needy among us. Money is for enjoyment and celebration. You can't just be paying bills and not enjoy the fruit of your labour.

TEN KEYS TO WIN WITH MONEY

1. Become an excellent <u>earner</u>: You cannot manage what you don't have. Study income generation. Aim for a minimum of 3 income streams.
2. Simplify your lifestyle so that you can live on less than you make.
3. <u>Track</u> your money. Know where it all goes. Live on a <u>budget</u>.
4. Be an excellent <u>Manager</u>: What you don't manage well you lose/waste. Manage money <u>God's Way</u>: God is the owner of everything.
5. Management means having a <u>system or plan</u> that enables you to give, spend, save and invest.
6. Separate your money and <u>assign</u> each amount to <u>specific purposes</u>.
7. Become <u>Generous</u>: Excel in the grace of giving: After taking care of yourself and family, this is the next goal.
8. Give and save <u>before</u> you spend. Get proper investment advice from experts.
9. <u>Eliminate Debt</u> as much as possible: The borrower is slave to the lender. Debt hinders generosity.
10. Build wealth <u>legitimately</u> but don't be a rich fool.

Your income is your greatest wealth building tool. Having an income is vital to your survival. If you do not earn, you cannot eat or pay your bills. If you are not earning, someone else is earning so you can live. Earning does not necessarily mean having a 9-to-5 job or waiting on a salary at the end of the month, because even children can earn. It means finding a way to be compensated monetarily for your service. It is monetizing your service.

Money is a mere compensation in paper or coin for a service. Jim Rohn, American business philosopher and my favourite personal development teacher, would say, "profits are better than wages." You can make a profit without waiting to be paid weekly, fortnightly or monthly. Most successful persons have at least three income streams. Most poor people have only one.

MILLIONAIRE MONEY MANAGEMENT SYSTEMS

The systems highlighted in this section have made the proponents wealthy. The aim is to expose you to different ways of managing money and encourage you to create, modify or adopt one of them so that you too can win with money. Winning with money is a matter of *proper* management. Proper management requires discipline, sacrifice and consistency with clear long-term goals in mind and the development of a plan.

DAVE RAMSEY'S MONEY MAP

Dave Ramsey's story is one of riches to bankruptcy to riches again. In the early 1990s, Ramsey made some

MILLIONAIRE MONEY MAP

Dave Ramsey's **The Seven Baby Steps**

Baby Step 1
$1,000 cash in a beginner emergency fund

Baby Step 2
Use the debt snowball to pay off all your debt but the house

Baby Step 3
A fully funded emergency fund of 3 to 6 months of expenses

Baby Step 4
Invest 15% of your household income into retirement

Baby Step 5
Start saving for college

Baby Step 6
Pay off your home early

Baby Step 7
Build wealth and give generously

bad financial decisions and became heavily indebted. Ramsey had a young family, and during this time, he became a Christian and learnt principles from the Bible to manage his money. The main principle he learnt at that time was: "the borrower is slave to the lender." Dave, having experienced this personally, began to wage war on debt. Over the last 25 years, he has enabled millions of people to get out of debt through his book, *Total Money Makeover*, his FINANCIAL PEACE UNIVERSITY, (a 9-week financial course) and *The Dave Ramsey Show*.

Dave has succeeded in changing his financial family tree, and now one of his daughters has joined him in the war on debt. The Ramsey show is a daily three-hour broadcast, which is aired on 500 radio stations in the USA, Canada and other countries. Each week, he has a millionaire themed hour where millionaires share their journey. There is also an exciting "Debt Free Scream" segment, where persons who have gotten out of debt come to share their story and make their debt free scream.

These are truly exciting and inspiring initiatives which give people hope of winning with money. Dave Ramsey's company Ramsey Solutions now employs over 400 people. He has truly turned tragedy into triumph, and now he teaches people to plan holistically for their financial success. Ramsey teaches seven (7) "Baby Steps" which must be followed sequentially to eliminate debt and build wealth. However, steps 4-6 can be done together:

Baby Step 1: US$1,000 cash in a beginner emergency fund. Do whatever it takes to save this portion. This often means finding a way to earn more, getting a second job or selling things that are not absolutely needed. This should be done as quickly as possible. Doing this first prevents you from going back into debt for little emergencies and acts as a buffer.

Baby Step 2: Use the debt snowball to pay off all of your debt but the house. This means listing all debts from smallest to largest and attacking them in that order using income from your second job, other earning initiatives or sale of assets.

Baby Step 3: A fully funded emergency fund of 3 to 6 months of expenses.

Baby Step 4: Invest 15% of your household income into retirement.

Baby Step 5: Start saving for college.

Baby Step 6: Pay off your home early.

Baby Step 7: Build wealth and give generously.

Note well: Ramsey's plan calls for a simplification of your lifestyle and tremendous sacrifice.

It means working hard and living on "rice and beans" until the debt is cleared. This is why Ramsey's mantra is "Live Like No One Else." Investment should only be done after *Baby Step 3*. Ramsey's plan prohibits borrowing for anything except the purchase of a house.

T. HARVEY EKER'S MONEY MAP

T. Harvey Eker is the author of the book, *Secrets of the Millionaire Mind* (2005). Harvey's story is one of those "rags to riches" stories, and while I don't embrace Harvey's spirituality, his money management system has enabled many to win with money, and I believe it is worth sharing. Harvey's plan, unlike Ramsey's, does not put your life on hold for say 18-24 months while you focus on debt reduction. This means that you may be indebted for a longer period while you focus on working towards financial freedom. Financial freedom is the ability to live off the income from your investments without working in the traditional sense. It is a plan which enables you to retire early or live a retired life, where you work by choice rather than necessity. Eker uses the concept of six jars. These could be literal jars, envelopes or bank accounts which are categorized as follows:

- Financial Freedom Account (FFA) = 10%
- Long Term Savings for Spending (LTSS) = 10%
- Education (EDUC) = 10%
- Necessities (NEC) =55%
- Play = 10%
- Give = 5%

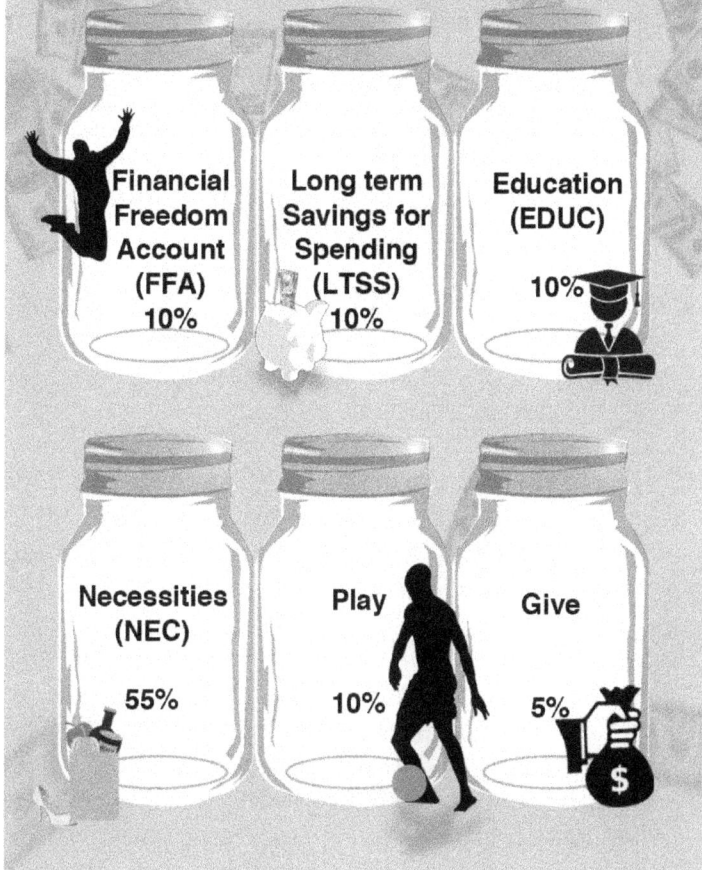

MILLIONAIRE MONEY MAP

T. Harvey Eker -
The Six Jars

Below is the explanation of the Eker's Jars system:

1. Put 55% of your income into NEC or Necessities: rent, food, gas, bills, debts etc.

2. 10% in Long-Term Savings for Spending, other-wise known as the rainy-day fund. Or maybe there's a car, house or some other big expense factor. Identify the item you want to buy and save towards it. This fund is your most flexible in terms of what you can do with it. It also serves as your emergency fund. I recommend bearing in mind Ramsey's Bay Steps 1 and 3 for this category.

3. 10% for Play. This is for leisurely expenses in-cluding sports, movies, general activity and en-tertainment. Eker recommends spending ALL your play money each month spoiling yourself!

4. 10% for Education. This is an investment in your personal growth or self-development such as books, courses, mentoring, coaching, etc. Al-ways educate yourself.

5. 10% for FFA or Financial Freedom Account. This is for investing or anything that is going to make this portion of your money work for you toward passive income streams.

6. 5% for Giving. It's a spiritually, ethically, and morally sound practice to give a portion of your earnings toward causes that can use the funding to educate or somehow better other people's lives. I however think, that it would be better to allot 10% here. The more you give, the more you receive. This would mean reducing your education percentage to 5%.

Harvey emphasizes that what matters most on this journey is not the amount of money you start with but building a habit. You could start this plan with a mere J$100 or US$100, and then it will be easier to manage your monthly salary or regular earnings.

Jim Rohn's Money Map

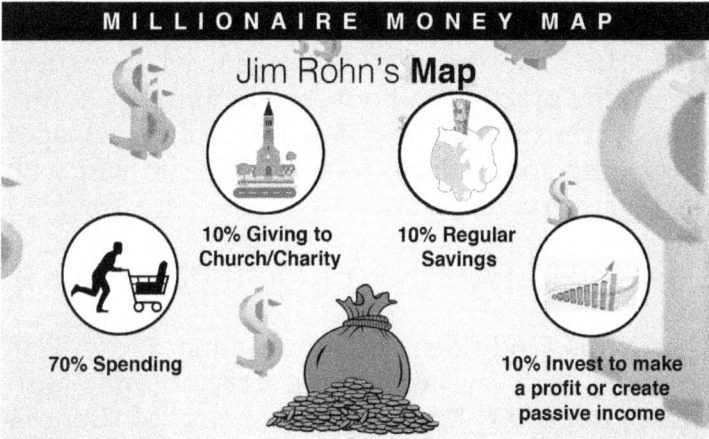

The late Jim Rohn was an American business philosopher, author and motivational speaker. His is another rags to riches story, in which a poor farm boy from Idaho became a millionaire and great influencer in his generation by following the principles taught by his mentor, Mr. Earl Shoaff. Rohn, a family man, was broke at age 25 and by age 31, he was a millionaire. Then he went broke again after some bad money decisions but was able to recover and become a millionaire for good. Jim Rohn in his presentation, "A Child and a Dollar," advocated a 70:10:10:10 principle.

- 70% - Spending
- 10% - Giving to Church/Charity
- 10% - Regular Savings

- 10% - Invest to make a profit or create passive income.

Rohn taught children to become thrifty. Instead of asking for one bicycle at Christmas, ask for two: one to ride and one to rent. His advice for adults who are highly indebted was to vary the percentages. This may mean 97:1:1:1. Again what matters here is the practice and not the amount. Jim Rohn's plan is an excellent way to teach money management even to children, so that they can win with money from an early age.

THE FAMINE PROOF PLAN

The name and idea of the Famine Proof Plan emerged from my study of the story of Prime Minister Joseph of Egypt in the book of Genesis chapters 37-41, as I prepared to teach the series on financial management at my friend's church. I believe it was a Divine insight and a specific directive and strategy for me to win with money.

According to the biblical story, God gave Pharaoh by way of two dreams advanced notice of a seven year famine and a seven year period of abundance. Pharaoh did not understand the dream, and Joseph, who was then imprisoned on false charges of rape, was invited to interpret his dream.

Joseph had a gift for interpreting dreams accurately. He interpreted the dream and then had the wisdom to give Pharaoh a strategy to prepare for the years of famine and secure Egypt's economic system. This plan pleased Pharaoh, and it resulted in Joseph being promoted to Prime Minister of Egypt.

Egypt's economy depended on agriculture. Joseph shared a simple plan. He told them to store away

1/5th of the grain for 7 years during the period of abundance. They followed his advice and, when the period of famine became severe, he opened the store houses and sold the grain to the people in Egypt and those who came from other countries. In this way, Egypt prospered in a time of prolonged disaster and became the main supplier of food for the next 7 years. Application and Lessons

THE FAMINE-PROOF PLAN

10% - Giving

20% FPP

5% Emergency, special needs and projects

55% - Spending for regular expenses

5% - Education

5% - Play

Save 20% of your income for 7 years. Begin investing in the 7th year. Use money to make a profit.

Wealth Building: The Famine Proof Plan is not just a mere rainy day plan to survive in brief periods of disaster or difficult economic times. It is a profit-making, wealth building plan to thrive and flourish during extended periods of economic down turn. It can be used as a retirement plan and as a financial legacy plan. When applied to our earnings, it is an excellent strategy to win with money. To implement this plan, you need a sustained 7-year period of plenty; that is, a period of steady and ongoing income generation. From this income, save 20% and continue doing so for 7 years without touching it.

Profit-Making: At the end of the period of saving, utilize some of the funds to make a profit. Identify a specific need to be met and see how you can create a sellable product which people will purchase to meet that need. You could also invest in instruments to make a profit but make certain you seek expert investment advice before you invest. Additionally, do not deplete your fund. You could continue repeating the process as long as you live and are able to earn or generate income.

The Famine Proof Plan is an excellent way to fast track your wealth, especially if you are a recent graduate who is just entering the workforce but without any debt. If I knew about it then, I would have been wealthy already. I graduated without debt but mostly spent my salary on one thing or another in my early years. This is one of my regrets. The Famine Proof Plan can help you to make up for lost years, if you are willing to sacrifice to do it.

If you were to save 20% of an income of J$120,000 per month, that would be J$24,000 per month towards your FFP account. At the end of the year, you would have J$288,000. In seven years, you would have J$2,016,000—over 2 million dollars. That's more than most persons save in a lifetime, and that is just based on one income stream. If you create other streams, the effect is magnified. Here are two versions of the Famine Proof Plan using a modification of Rohn's plan and Eker's plan:

FPP Version 1:

10% - Giving
20% - FFP

10% - Saving for emergency, special needs and projects
60% - Spending for regular expenses

FPP Version 1:

10% - Giving
20% - FFP
5% - Emergency, special needs and projects
55% - Spending for regular expenses
5% - Education
5% - Play

Now which one of these money management systems do you prefer? Choose one and start winning with money today.

CREDIT CARD ADVISORY

"There is nothing so useless as doing efficiently that which should not be done at all."
—Peter Drucker

I could not close this segment without doing a feature on credit cards. Credit card mismanagement has been one of my regrets, and I am educating as many persons as possible about the need to be careful with credit cards.

According to Dr. Myles Munroe, "The reason we are in trouble is because of <u>mismanagement</u> through greed." In his book *Overcoming Crisis,* he defines management as "the effective, efficient, correct, and timely use of another person's property and resources for the purpose for which they were delegated with a view to producing the expected added value" (2015, 39).

I know that definition of management is a mouthful. It makes me shriek when I consider the mismanagement of my credit card, and sadly I am not alone. Credit card debt is one of the leading causes of bankruptcy. My goal here is to briefly expose some of the hidden dangers of credit card fees which come with mismanagement, so that I can help you to become a better steward of a credit card or to eventually surrender the "need" for one.

Once you have a credit card and depending on how many you have, it can become quite burdensome. If you are only making minimum payments, you have just added a "utility bill" to your list of monthly expenses. You will have a recurring monthly fee, which if not paid will result in fines. Sadly, unlike the electric company, cable company or water commission, credit card companies will not cut your service for non-payment. They will let the charges increase ad infinitum. In this regard, the credit card becomes a strict teacher in the school of discipline.

Having one or more credit cards is an excellent way to be schooled in the art of *discipline:* the discipline of paying attention to and monitoring your deadlines and exercising control over your impulses. Trust me, the pain of mismanagement will teach you how to be vigilant like no other teacher! When deadlines are missed, you are in trouble! And when you fail to keep your spending impulse in check, there will be "hell" to pay in fees: anxiety, depression, insomnia hypertension and the like, and sadly bankruptcy and even suicide in some cases.

A credit card is a psychological trap. One of the reasons so many businesses are going cashless is that when you use a card, you do not feel it until the bill comes. When you spend hard cash, it is reported; this activates the pain centre in the brain, but paperless transactions like a credit card do not. If you are not careful, you will purchase many little items online and elsewhere, and only when the bill comes do you feel the (delayed) pain. In addition, the use of the card may prevent you from bargaining or negotiating for a lowered price or good deal. After all, who negotiates with a computer, card machine or Amazon online?

"HIDDEN" FEES

I mean fees that you did not readily think of when you were getting the card or fees the credit card sales person never explained to you or highlighted. In many cases, the emphasis is only on two payments: the minimum fee and the annual user fee. Bear in mind that "fees" mean money you are or may be liable to pay to the credit company. These fees in many cases do not decrease your principal loan nor need to be paid any time at all. The only way to avoid most of these penalties is to make sure you pay the card in full on time each month and never lose the card. This is especially so if you have a card with an annual fee.

The following lists 15 possible credit card fees based on National Commercial Bank (NCB) rates and charges in 2016. This information came in a brochure sent to me by mail from NCB. Pay close attention to the percentages, and I will provide a few practical examples of the implications. The results will shock you!

I am using my MasterCard as an example. However, all the other cards like Classic Keycard, Lovebird Keycard, Gold Keycard, Travel Mastercard, etc.

have the same categories of charges though the amount varies.

1. Primary Joining/Annual Fee - US$90.00
2. Supplementary Annual Fees - US$60.00
3. Replacement Card Fee -US$60.00
4. Annual Interest rate [Unsecured] - 18% -21%
5. Annual Interest rate [Secured] - 15%
6. Cash Advance Fee at NCB Branch - 10% plus GCT
7. Cash Advance Fee at ABM - 7.3% plus GCT
8. Over Limit Fee - US$69.00
9. Late Payment Fee - US$69.00
10. Returned Cheque - US$65.00
11. Replacement Statement - US$20.00
12. Credit Report [per report] - US$55.00
13. Credit Bureau Fee - J$2105.16
14. Voucher Search/Item Retrieval - per item (at cardholder's request) - US$25.00
15. Monthly Minimum Payment - 4% of monthly statement balance

Tell the truth! If you already have a credit card, were you aware of all possible charges when you signed up? I sure was not! Furthermore, do you see the danger of #15, which is exactly how the bank wants you to make you a credit card slave?

Note Well: In Jamaica, we do not operate in US dollars. Each month, a Jamaican will pay a different amount based on the fluctuation of the Jamaican dollar upon conversion. You lose if your primary currency is not the same as the credit card.

SAM'S STORY

User Fee: Sam has a US Dollar MasterCard with a limit of $1000.00. Let's say he has had his card for 10 years and only paid the annual user fee. This means Sam either paid the card in full whenever he used it or he never used it. If the user fee remains at $60.00 for 10 years, Sam has given the credit card company US$600 to retain/ use the card. It is likely that the cost would have increased in those years as well.

What if Sam gave up the card in year three and had an emergency fund of US$1000? Sam would have saved at least US$420, which he could have invested elsewhere. *Now is it really worth it, Sam?* No wonder Steven Covey says effective people have the habit of starting with the end in mind. I say think long term to win!

Minimum Payments and Other Fees: Imagine Sam had a medical emergency and maxed out his card, and for some reason, he resorted to paying only the minimum payments for 10 years. He would automatically have been giving the credit card company more money.

4% of 1000 is 40; 40 x10 = 400

Now add the annual user fee of $600 for 10 years. In 10 years, Sam would have paid the credit card company at least US$1000, and his credit card principal would remain untouched. *He still owes them US$1000!*

The situation is even more frightening if Sam missed payments, paid the minimum payment late during those years and made a cash advance/withdrawal. His balance would have increased, and he would have had to give more money to the bank than he originally borrowed. By now, you get the point. *Is it really worth it, Sam?*

I have been Sam, and there are many Sams out there! I hope that you are seeing the insanity of it all. If you do need to have a credit card, bear in mind the responsibilities, and do not become a victim of stupid taxation through mismanagement.

QUESTIONS TO PONDER

Having delineated the above, honestly answer the following questions:

a) Do you still want a credit card?
b) If so, are you only making minimum payments?
c) Have you been paying your credit card on time?
d) Do you have credit card regrets?
e) Is it worth keeping a credit card?
f) Can you really manage this responsibility?
g) Is there a better way to do your business without a credit card?

WINNING WITH MONEY
RESOURCE MATERIALS

Total Money Makeover, Dave Ramsey
The Millionaire Next Door, Thomas J. Stanley and
    William D. Danko
Secrets of the Millionaire Mind, T. Harvey Eker
The Richest Man in Babylon, George Samuel Clason

Think and Grow Rich, Napoleon Hill
The Legacy Journey, Dave Ramsey
Smart Money Smart Kids, Dave Ramsey and Rachel
   Cruze

Disclaimer: I do not subscribe to all philosophies shared in these books. However, they do contain some practical wisdom, which anyone can apply to win with money. I discard anything that does not align with my Christian faith. "Examine everything carefully; hold fast to that which is good" (I Thessalonians 5:21).

CHAPTER 17:
DO IT

*"To have a plan and not act
on it is futile."*
—Myles Munroe

This brief final chapter covers Step 5 of the *Design to Win* process ("Do It"). Let me remind you that this book is ultimately about life-change, and life-change does not come by mere dreaming and wishing or even planning. Life-change comes when we take action and act consistently to implement our plans.

In 2017, one of my FIT members in his 5-minute inspirational segment (I usually have a motivational segment at the beginning or end of the session) shared a quote which I will never forget. He said, "When all is said and done, more is said than done." Do not let this be true of you, especially after reading the past sixteen (16) chapters. In Jamaica we say "action, not a bag a mouth." It's time for action! Do not let my stories of regret and recommendations for change go in vain.

To further help you on your journey to living an effective or winning life and career, I have a created a mini Design to Win toolkit for you in Appendix A. It has some resources which can change your life as well as winning job-hunting tips. These tips are for those of you who will need to get your first job or a new job to pursue the career path you love, and work for significance rather than mere survival.

As this book comes to a close, let me remind you of the five (5) proven steps to win in your life and career:

Step 1, Discovery: Do a self-inventory to become more aware of your skills, talents and desires. Study and analyze your life to see where you have been, where you are now and where you would like to go. Find out in this phase—for those who are persons of faith—the will of your Divine Designer.

Step 2, Decision-Making: Make a decision regarding your purpose and your major life and career goals, especially for the next 1-5 years. Create holistic goals.

Step 3, Design: Devise a strategic action plan to achieve your major life and career goals over the next 5 years. Use the sample life and career plan provided as a guide.

Step 4, Development: Learn some key interpersonal and life-management skills to create a winning life and career and bring your design to life. These include the Art of Life Hurdling, how to deal with failure and rejection and the management of your time and money. Ongoing learning will be vital, and this can be done formally and informally.

Step 5, Do It: Take action and do it consistently despite the odds to accomplish your major life and career goals. Find or create a fulfilling job. Learn to be properly compensated for doing work you love. Persevere and never give up.

Remember: no matter how bad it is or how bad it gets, YOU CAN STILL WIN! Follow these steps, use the resources in the toolkit and go astonish the world! Go create a winning life and career! Live purposefully and effectively!

APPENDIX A:
THE DESIGN TO WIN
TOOLKIT

The majority of young people upon leaving high school will require further training before entering the working world. Once you figure out your next step (through further studies or work), the information shared here will be vital. Remember what Jim Rohn says: "Formal education will make you a living but self-education will make you a fortune." Don't stop learning, be it formal or informal.

SELF-DEVELOPMENT

"If you wish to achieve worthwhile things in your personal and career life, you must become a worthwhile person in your own self-development."
—Brian Tracy

Recommended Books and Audios

These recommended resources include my own books, the Bible and other resources which have helped to transform my life. I don't subscribe to all the teachings/views expressed by all the authors or presenters, but I gained valuable insights and principles that helped to change different areas of my life. Take the meat and throw away the bones. Some of these resources are on YouTube; others are on Amazon. These are not in alphabetical order.

Books

The Magic of Thinking Big, Dr. David Schwartz
Focal Point, Brian Tracy
The Psychology of Achievement, Brian Tracy
The Winning Attitude, John Maxwell
Failing Forward, John Maxwell
Keys to Win at Life, C. Ruth Taylor
When Trees Talk, Cameka I. Taylor
Heartache Queen Unshackled, Cameka I. Taylor
What Colour is Your Parachute? 2018 Edition,
    Richard Bolles
Feel the Fear but Do it Anyway, Dr. Susan Jeffers
Eat that Frog, Brian Tracy
Disappointment with God, Philip Yancey

YouTube Channels/Podcasts

Blake. Roberto. Always Be Creating. https://www-
    .youtube.com/user/robertoblake2
Carmichael, Evan. Believe.
    https://www.youtube.com/user/Modeling-
    TheMasters
Flynn, Pat. Smart Passive Income. https://www-
    .smartpassiveincome.com/
Howes, Lewis. The School of Greatness. https://-
    www.youtube.com/user/lewishowes
Hyatt, Michael. Lead to Win.
    https://michaelhyatt.com/leadtowin/

Hogan, Chris. Retired Inspired.
   https://www.chrishogan360.com/
Ramsey, Dave. The Ramsey Show. https://www-
   .youtube.com/user/DaveRamseyShow/
Savelle-Foy, Terri. Live Your Dreams. https://-
   www.youtube.com/user/terrisavellefoy

Scholarship Opportunities

If you are considering formal studies and lack the resources check out the following three resource platforms:

Embassies in Your Country. Many scholarships are not seized due to ignorance.

For Jamaicans: Check Scholarship Jamaica. This site lists scores of scholarships and has been operational since 2001. https://scholarshipja-maica.com/

Internationally: The World Scholarship Forum. http://worldscholarshipforum.com/

WINNING 21ST CENTURY JOB-HUNTING TIPS

Many of these tips are adapted from the world's leading career expert for over 40 years, Richard "Dick" Bolles who passed away in March 2017. His book, *What Colour is Your Parachute?*, was updated annually and read by more than 10 million people and translated into some 26 languages. May these 10 tips help you to land a job you will love!

1. **Self-Study/Self-Inventory:** Figure out your preference in seven areas:

   a) favourite working conditions
   b) preferred kinds of people to work with
   c) what you can do and love to do (transferrable skills)
   d) your favourite knowledges or fields of interest
   e) preferred salary and level of responsibility
   f) preferred places to live and preferred geographical factors
   g) your major goal/purpose, values or philosophy in life

Understanding these preferences will position you to approach employers as a valuable resource instead of as a beggar.

2. **Links:** Use "Links" or bridge persons to make contact with the organization or the prospective employer. These are persons that know you and the hiring managers at the company of interest. Most jobs are secured in this way.

3. **Circles of influence:** Use your circles to spread the word. As Dick Bolles says "job-hunting requires 80 pairs of eyes." Involve friends, family and acquaintances from school, church clubs online and offline.

4. **Think Beyond the Résumé:** Don't rely on your résumé alone to get you the job. Its purpose is to get you to the interview. Make sure it is done properly. It is how you perform at the interview which often determines whether you get the

job or not. Google is the new resume. Make sure you think before you "selfie" as employers are watching your social media foot print. Use social media to your advantage to market yourself instead of ruining your chance of finding your dream job.

5. **Think Like An Employer:** Know what employers are looking for and how they search for employees.

6. **Research:** Research the company thoroughly before you approach them, you don't have to wait for a vacancy before applying. Go in and conduct informational interviews with company staff if possible. Present yourself as a resource. This works especially with smaller companies with 50 or less employees.

7. **Interview Preparation:** Practice well for your interview and groom yourself appropriately.

8. **Online Job-Hunting:** Make use of LinkedIn, company websites and employment sites. Use Linkedin to network as well. Here are four online job-hunting sites for Jamaicans or Caribbean persons:

- Caribbean Jobs, https://www.caribbeanjobs-.com/
- Splash Jamaica, http://www.splashjamaica.-com/
- Go Jamaica Job Smart, http://go-jamaica.com/jobsmart/

9. **A Blended Approach:** use a variety of techniques. Do not rely on one means. For example, simply sending out résumés to companies and then sit at home waiting for a response.

10. **Time and Perseverance:** Invest time and persevere. Job-hunting can be a long process fraught with much rejection. Keep going and do spend more than one hour per week searching. Treat your search like a 9-to-5 job, five days per week, until you find employment.

A 21st Century Work Tip

Given the nature of the 21st century with an increase in technology, robotics and the rise of the internet, more and more people will be working from home. There is renewed emphasis on entrepreneurship and personal job creation for greater freedom, flexibility and fulfillment. Many jobs will become extinct and new jobs will be created. It's time to think like an entrepreneur.

Know this: 85% of start-ups fail. Thus, while you grow your business, you more than likely will need either a part-time or full-time job to sustain yourself and or family. Job-hunting will still be relevant as you seek to grow your own business. The first tip shared is not just for job-hunting but also for choosing a career. The self-study results may lead to you to become an entrepreneur or work for someone else.

APPENDIX B: CAREER AND LIFE EMPOWERMENT INITIATIVES

DESIGN TO WIN ACADEMY

The Design to Win Academy is our primary platform for career and life-management initiatives to empower youths and Go-Getters. 80% of our services are offered online. The main services offered are:

- Workshops and Courses in career and life planning or life management. These are conducted Online and Face to Face (Live)
- Career and Life Empowerment Talks
- Job-Hunting Consultation: Résumé review, job-hunting tips and interview preparation
- Career Coaching/Consultation

Some of the courses and workshops include:

- Design to Win Fundamentals
- The Art of Life Hurdling
- Millionaire Money Maps
- Setting Smart Goals
- Winning Job-Hunting Strategies
- Keys to Win at Life

We have single session workshops for one hour or more hours; one day workshops and weekend workshop series depending on the need. There are mini 5-day email courses as well as standard 4-6 weeks online courses. There are also face to face intensive courses held over weekends.

THE FIT PROGRAM

This is a faith-based youth mentoring, coaching and leadership training programme to raise up Future Innovators (cycle breakers and world changers) who will learn the keys to win at life and pass them on to others. The programme usually lasts 6 to 18 months depending on the need of the group. The FIT program teaches youths 16-34 years of age key strategies to flourish in time. It offers career guidance and life management principles to help them create winning lives and careers.

Our vision is to raise up 10, 000 Innovators who will learn, change and pass on the keys to win at life. The FIT program emphasizes personal, spiritual and professional development (body, soul and spirit) as part of the strategy to be FIT for life. The minimum number of participants for this programme is (8) eight.

CAREER AND LIFE PLANNING FAIRS OR JOB FAIRS

These are done in partnership with churches, schools and communities.

BEHIND THESMILE

This is our flagship personal development and inspirational live event targeting primarily young professionals and young adults. It is a forum where successful persons, groups or organizations share their stories, mixed with a talent showcase, a Keys to Success workshop and tips to help people get their smile back. The event also showcases causes to be supported. TheSmile is a symbol of triumph, hope, transformation and success, and these characteristics represent our mission for the event.

CONTACT INFORMATION:

Join the Design to Win Academy or contact Extra MILE Innovators (EMI) for career and life empowerment initiatives. EMI is a personal and professional coaching and training business which creates initiatives to Motivate, Inspire, Liberate and Empower (MILE) people to win at life. EMI was founded by C. Ruth Taylor in 2015 as part of her thrust to go the extra mile with the "extra time" God gave her to exalt Him and empower people.

Contact us for more information:

Email: ruthtaylor@extramileja.com | extramileinnovators@gmail.com
Telephone: (1876) 782-9896
Website: www.extramileja.com | www.designtowinacademy.com

Subscribe to our Design to Win YouTube channel and our Facebook community.

DESIGN TO WIN
DTW
ACADEMY
SERVICES
Contact us for any of the following career and life management services:
Workshops and courses Online/face to face
Empowerment talks and events
Job-hunting consultation
Mentoring, career coaching and personal development training
Career and Life Planning/Job Fairs

GRATEFUL ACKNOWLEDGEMENTS

I am grateful to God, my Life Designer, for teaching me by His example how to Design to Win. This book further owes a debt of gratitude to Tedecia Powell-Coley, through whom I discovered my love for career development and life skills. Thanks for playing such a vital role in my professional development.

To my immediate family, thanks for motivating me to write and for wholeheartedly investing in the vision to change lives.

To members of my Design to Win Facebook community who provided the necessary feedback to refine the book; of whom special mention must be made of Sheril Morgan, Didan Ashanta, Susan Muir, Jo-Ann Richards-Goffe, Paulette McKenzie-Williams, Rohan King, and all who took the time to provide much needed feedback during the production process. To members of my FIT team and Butterfly 276, thanks for your feedback in refining the publishing package.

To participants of my Design to Win online and face to face courses and those who participated in workshops and coaching initiatives, thanks for encouraging me to take this message to more people. Special thanks to Rev. Dr. Carla Dunbar for enlisting persons to do the Design to Win Fundamentals course. I'm forever grateful.

To Mrs. Faith Thomas, thanks for your wonderful endorsement and encouragement.

To my publishing team: N.D. Author Services [NDAS]; Norman Cooper, illustrator; thanks for transforming mere words into a very desirable package.

ABOUT THE AUTHOR

Cameka "Ruth" Taylor is an educator, certified career coach, author and speaker from the beautiful island of Jamaica. She is also the creator of the *Design to Win* Academy (a virtual career and life management institute) and Extra MILE Innovators (a personal and professional development business).

As a career coach, Ruth helps Budding and Young Professionals to discover their purpose and passion and redesign their lives to find/create a fulfilling career. Since 2010, she has helped scores of people to successfully redesign their lives and careers for greater effectiveness, fulfillment and joy.

With over 15 years of speaking experience, Ruth has been empowering thousands of people in Jamaica, countries in the wider Caribbean, Latin America and Africa to win in their personal, professional and spiritual lives.

Ruth's qualifications include a Diploma in Teaching, a B.A in General Studies, a Masters in Theology and a Career Coaching Certificate. *Design to Win Road Map* is her 4th published book since March 2015.

REFERENCES

Anderson, Neil T. *Victory Over the Darkness. Bethany House.* 2000.

Bolles, Richard. *What Colour is Your Parachute?* 2018 Edition. Ten Speed Press, 2018.

Clarke, Helen. *The UNDP Caribbean Human Development Report 2012.* http://www.undp.org/content/dam/undp/library/.../C_bean_HDR_Jan25_2012_3MB.pdf

Covey, Stephen. *The 7 Habits of Highly Effective People.* Rosetta Book, 2013.

Duhigg, Charles. *The Power of Habits.* Random House, 2014.

Eker, T. Harvey. *Secrets of the Millionaire Mind.* Harper Business,2005.

Hyatt, Michael. *This is your Life Podcast.* Web. https://michaelhyatt.com/thisisyourlife

McCormack, Mark. *What they Don't Teach You in the Harvard Business School.* Bantam, 1986.

Munroe, Myles. *Overcoming Crisis.* Destiny Image, 2015.

Ramsey, Dave. *The Total Money Makeover.* Thomas Nelson, 2009.

Schwartz, David. *The Magic of Thinking Big.* Fireside, 1987.

Statistical Institute of Jamaica (STATIN). *Population Statistics: Total End of Year Population by Age and Sex.* Web. March 31, 2018. http://statinja.gov.jm/Demo_SocialStats/PopulationStats.aspx

Supreme Court of Jamaica. *Statistical Report for the Parish Courts of Jamaica.* Web. March 31, 2017. http://supremecourt.gov.jm/sites/default/files/-FIRST-QUARTER-STATISTICAL-REPORT-ON-CRIMINAL-MATTERS-IN-THE-PARISH-COURTS.pdf.

The Manpower Group. *Millennial Careers: 2020 Vision.* Web. https://www.manpowergroup-.com/wps/.../MillennialsPaper1_2020Vision_lo.pdf?. 2016

Tracy, Brian. *Eat That Frog.* Berrett-Koehler Publishers, 2007.

_____. *Reinvention.* AMACOM, 2009.

OTHER PUBLICATIONS

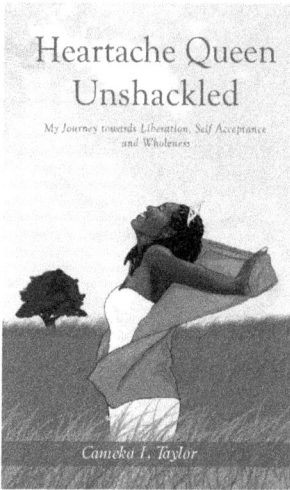

Heartache Queen Unshackled

This is a teaching autobiography about overcoming fear, relational heartaches and pain and finding emotional wholeness. This book will help you to find liberation and healing.

Trade Paperback, ISBN: 978-976-8240-23-1

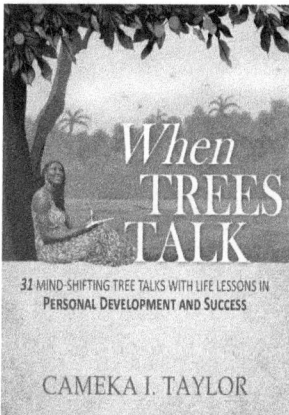

When Trees Talk

This is a series of 31 motivational talks with 100 life lessons to release the winning you. This is your daily dose of motivation to keep you on the winning path when discouraged.

Trade Paperback, ISBN: 978-1-62676-914-4

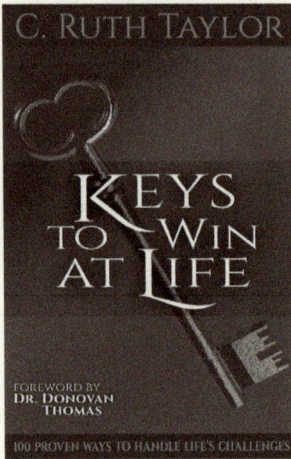

Keys to Win at Life

This is a success tool-kit of one hundred proven success strategies to effectively handle everyday life challenges. The book has 100 real life applications and 100 proverbs to help you to live an effective life. This book will help you to progress in life.

Trade Paperback, ISBN: 978-1-62676-891-7